DARKROOM

WYNN BULLOCK
JERRY BURCHARD
LINDA CONNOR
LARRY CLARK
RALPH GIBSON
BETTY HAHN
EIKOH HOSOE
GEORGE KRAUSE
ELAINE MAYES
DUANE MICHALS
W. EUGENE SMITH
GEORGE TICE
JERRY UELSMANN

EDITED BY ELEANOR LEWIS

LUSTRUM PRESS

LIBRARY OF CONGRESS CATALOG CARD NUMBER: 76-57201

ISBN: CLOTH 0-912810-20-3 • PAPER 0-912810-19-x

TYPOGRAPHY BY HAROLD BLACK INC. • PRINTED BY RAPOPORT PRINTING CORPORATION

DISTRIBUTED BY LIGHT IMPRESSIONS CORPORATION, BOX 3012, ROCHESTER, NEW YORK

PHYSICAL FACT/PSYCHIC EFFECT

I would like to express my gratitude first of all to the photographers included here for their continued and invaluable support of this project. Also thanks to David Mancini of Photopia Gallery, Philadelphia, Mrs Edna Bullock and Jim Hill for their contributions to the chapters by George Krause and Wynn Bullock. Finally, a heartfelt thanks to my partners at Lustrum Press, John Flattau, Ralph Gibson and Arne Lewis who have been most generous with their advice, skills and time. E.L.

In our daily lives we are bombarded with photographs. They leap out at us from the pages of our newspapers and magazines, from billboards on the highway, from junk mail that arrives every morning. The sheer number of pictures to which we are exposed is overwhelming. We cease to take them in. Artists who choose the camera as their means of expression risk being absorbed unless their statements have sufficient impact. The content of a photograph is almost always determined at the time of exposure. But it can be strengthened and refined or even destroyed in the darkroom. This potential for success or failure makes darkroom technique of prime importance to any photographer.

Here is a group of photographers who have been brought together because they offer interesting points of view toward technique. It could be, for example, in the choice of an "obsolete" method of printing. George Tice, who can't buy the platinum papers he needs, makes his own and prints his large format negatives in the traditional way. Betty Hahn reinterprets the nineteenth-century process, Gum Printing, and creates new effects using color and multiple images. A photographer might use ordinary materials in an unusual way. Linda Connor prints her 8 x 10 negatives on Kodak studio proof, a paper customarily used by portrait photographers to make proofs for their clients. These proofs darken to a solid maroon on contact with light. But Connor makes her prints permanent and also gold tones them for a rich, gray-brown color. George Krause offers the formula and instruction for the use of a mecury intensifier which is no longer manufactured. He finds it an excellent solution to the problem of underexposed or underdeveloped negatives.

Although darkroom work is crucial to the art, the photographers represented here display a striking variety of feelings toward this aspect of their work. Some seem to enjoy it. Larry Clark says, "I like to print and have fun in the darkroom." Some do not. W. Eugene Smith says, "There's nothing I hate worse than the discipline of the darkroom . . ." Everyone agrees, however, that it is necessary. For instance, Smith goes on to say, ". . . and yet I have spent all these years printing. The reason is simple. I want the damn pictures to say what I want them to say." For this reason, he is also willing to spend tremendous amounts of time with a negative, even one that most people would throw out. Smith once spent five days and nights in the darkroom to get the print he was after.

Few are willing to go this far. Jerry Burchard rejects any negative which requires more than minimal burning and dodging. He feels that other negatives will be as good and sometimes even uses a machine, the I-Tek, to speed up the printing process. Duane Michals also dislikes the darkroom. Perhaps this is what motivated him to shift his emphasis toward the camera. His photographs deal mainly with situations where mood and emotions are suggested by lighting and in-camera effects such as blur and double exposure.

He sends his exposed film to a laboratory because he feels that once an idea has been captured, anyone can do an adequate job of printing. One might say that Michals has the world's smallest darkroom, his camera.

Jerry Uelsmann represents the other extreme. The most important part of his process takes place in the darkroom. Uelsmann practices a technique he calls "post visualization," the combining of several negatives to make a single print. His final statement results from juxtaposition and has little to do with the original images. Uelsmann's concept is one shared by many photographers, that of photograph as object. The image transcends its subject matter and becomes more than a record of what was photographed.

Bullock and several other photographers touch on what I consider to be a critical consideration, the need for a balance between craft and content. A photograph can be technically magnificent but meaningless if it lacks content.

Most of the photographers included in DARKROOM were interviewed and their spoken words edited into chapter form. In this way, I felt that the necessary technical information came across and the conversational tone seemed to encourage a communication of aesthetic and emotional attitudes. Those who wrote their own chapters included a discussion of these attitudes as well.

To introduce the artists, I have placed a brief biography at the beginning of each chapter. At the end of each chapter you will find a chart which summarizes technical information and, in some cases, supplements it. Scattered throughout the text are illustrations inserted to clarify procedure.

In photograpy books, photographs are generally the focus of the work. Here, this is not true. The pictures I have chosen are from the artists' better known work but they are intended to illustrate technical characteristics of style or to demonstrate the solutions to problems anybody might encounter.

DARKROOM is more than a "how to" book. It is a collection of statements on the role of craft and, as such, revealing on several levels. Much of the technical information is not available elsewhere, but more important, the flexibility of the materials and the possibility of breaking the rules successfully for specific reasons becomes apparent.

On the level of process, one sees the effort involved in pursuing this deceptively easy medium, the emotional difficulties to be fought through, the perseverence required. Basic photographic principles can be learned quickly. Instant results are possible. It is therefore helpful and comforting to be reminded that photography doesn't come easily even for the best. ELEANOR LEWIS, THETFORD HILL, VERMONT

WYNN BULLOCK

Wynn Bullock was born in Chicago in 1902. He attended school in South Pasadena, California, and moved to New York City in 1921 to prepare for a career as a singer. In 1928, he went to Paris to continue his studies, and concertized throughout France. Profoundly influenced by the work of Laszlo Moholy-Nagy and Man Ray, he began considering a career in photography.

Leaving Europe in 1931, Bullock went to live in Clarksburg, West Virginia where he attended the University of West Virginia as a pre-law student. In 1938, Bullock left law school and moved to California. He enrolled in the Los Angeles Art Center School to study photography under Edward Kaminski.

He began to freelance in 1940, and in 1942 enlisted in the Army. He was released to do photographic work in the aircraft industry in 1943. After the war, he traveled through California producing and selling post cards. In 1946, he settled in Monterey where he obtained the photographic concession for the Fort Ord military base and established a commercial photography business.

In 1948, after exhaustive research in solarization, he received patents in the United States, Canada, and Great Britain for a "Photographic Process for Producing Line Image." He met Edward Weston that same year, and was so affected by his photographs that he gave up experimental work and began taking "straight" photographs.

In 1955 Bullock's work was included in the "Family of Man" exhibition at the Museum of Modern Art in New York City, and the following year his photograph, LET THERE BE LIGHT, was voted the favorite by a majority of 65,000 viewers at the Corcoran Gallery of Art in Washington, D.C. In 1960, Bullock began work on color/light abstractions and continued to explore them until 1966, when he resumed black and white photography. In 1965, his first monograph, THE WIDENING STREAM (Peregrin Publications, Monterey, California) with text by Richard Mack, was published.

In 1968, he retired from commercial photography and in 1971, WYNN BULLOCK (The Scrimshaw Press, Oakland, California) appeared. This book won an award as one of the fifty best books of 1971 the American Institute of Graphic Arts. In 1973, WYNN BULLOCK PHOTOGRAPHY: A WAY OF LIFE (Morgan and Morgan, Dobbs Ferry, New York) was published.

From 1957 on, Bullock gave frequent seminars, lectures, and workshops. He was represented in over ninety group and one-man shows throughout his career. He received many awards for his work, and was widely published in magazines here and abroad.

Bullock's last published photograph was taken in 1973. In 1975, Bullock became one of five photographers to leave his archives to the Center for Creative Photography at the University of Arizona, Tucson. He died November 16, 1975.

His illustrated essay PHOTOGRAPH AS SYMBOL, A BOOK BY WYNN BULLOCK (Artichoke Press, Mountain View, California) was published posthumously.

Selected one-man exhibitions:

1941: Los Angeles County Museum

1956: M. H. de Young Museum, San Francisco
George Eastman House, Rochester, New York

1960: Princeton University, Graphic Arts Department, Princeton, New Jersey

1962: Carl Siembab Gallery, Boston

1964: University of Florida, Gainesville

1968: Rhode Island School of Design, Providence

1969: San Francisco Museum of Art
The Witkin Gallery, New York

1970: Amon Carter Museum of Western Art, Fort Worth, Texas

1972: de Saisett Art Gallery and Museum, University of Santa Clara, Santa Clara, California

1973: Bibliothèque Nationale, Paris

1974: Madison Art Center, Madison, Wisconsin
Focus Gallery, San Francisco

1972-1975: Royal Photographic Society, London
United States Information Agency traveling exhibition, Washington, D.C.

1976: Metropolitan Museum of Art, New York
The Art Institute of Chicago
San Francisco Museum of Art

Selected collections:
Bibliothèque Nationale, Paris
International Museum of Photography, George Eastman House, Rochester, New York
Metropolitan Museum of Art, New York
Museum of Modern Art, New York
National Gallery of Canada, Ottawa
Royal Photographic Society, London
San Francisco Museum of Art
Smithsonian Institution, Washington, D.C.
University of California at Los Angeles
Victoria and Albert Museum, London

Jim Hill

Wynn Bullock's darkroom

ABC PYRO DEVELOPER

Solution A:
sodium bisulfite — 140 grains
pyro — 2 ounces
potassium bromide — 16 grains
water to make — 32 ounces

Solution B:
water — 32 ounces
sodium sulfite — 3½ ounces

Solution C:
water — 32 ounces
sodium carbonate — 2½ ounces

Use fresh developer for each batch of film. For tray development, 1 part A, 1 part B, 1 part C and 7 parts water. Develop 6 minutes at 65 F. For tank development, take 9 ounces each of A, B and C and add water to make 1 gallon. Develop 12 minutes at 65 F. Remove any scum on surface of developer with blotting paper.

Figure 1.

From the beginning I have placed great emphasis on the fact that darkroom work is an important element in the creative photographic process. When photographing I become so involved in what I'm perceiving that I have to force myself to think of technique. I use a Weston meter, take a high and low reading, and bracket my exposures. My negatives aren't always what they should be, but that's the way it is.

I've gone through many aspects of photography. For eight years I did nothing but a technical study of solarization. Later I was granted patents in the United States, Great Britain, and Canada for a process controlling the line effect of solarization. I studied and practiced the Zone System. Finally I thought, "What the hell, it doesn't work unless I constantly test equipment and materials." I would rather spend my time concentrating on and reacting to the world about me. Of course, you gain a sense of technique by studying basics and working. I have a friend, Jim Hill, whose wife gave him a beautiful Weston Ranger meter. He used it for about a week and then threw it in the ocean. Something I don't recommend. He's got an eye for exposure and seldom makes errors. I don't have that good an eye, so I work with a meter.

From 1948 to 1960, I used an 8 x 10 Ansco View Camera with three lenses: a 10″ wide-field Ektar; a 14″ Ektar, and a 19″ Wollensak Process. I hand developed my negatives in a tray by inspection in ABC Pyro (Figure 1), but I found that I would occasionally scratch my negatives this way. Then a friend built me a nitrogen burst agitator which works beautifully. I usually gave two exposures so that if the first negative didn't come out well, I could vary the development of the second to produce the quality I wanted.

In the sixties, I started making color/light abstractions with an old 35mm Exakta camera and Kodachrome II Tungsten film. The 8 x 10 had become burdensome because of my age. Later I switched for general black and white work to an SL66 Rollei 2¼ camera and have been using it ever since. At first I didn't think I could produce the print quality I wanted, but when one puts one's mind to learning a technique, it soon becomes a practical tool. The developer I still use with 2¼ roll film is a modified Stockler developer: Solution A (metol — 10 grams, sodium sulphite — 150 grams, water — 2000 cc); Solution B (borax — 20 grams, water — 2000 cc); normal development is four and a half minutes in each at 70 F. This developer gives fine grain and plenty of latitude.

In printing, I now use Eastman Kodak Polycontrast paper, except for printing thin negatives which require high contrast papers. I use Brovira Nos. 5 or 6 for them. Fortunately, I don't have to use these contrasty papers too often because their latitude is limited. I develop in an Amidol developer (Figure 2) because I like the color it gives the print. The print is then toned in a selenium toner, given a hypo-clearing bath, and instead of the twenty minute recommended washing time, I wash it in an East Street Gallery Archival Washer for a minimum of one hour.

The first photograph I want to discuss is the POINT LOBOS TIDE POOL. This is a contact print from an 8 x 10 negative. The picture was taken at sunset and the light was dim. The sun was striking only the edges of the rocks in the upper-left-hand corner. The tide pool itself was especially dull, and the light was disappearing so fast I had to make a quick exposure. The negative is very soft (Figure 3), because in my hurry to capture the picture, I forgot to underexpose the film so that I could expand the contrast by overdeveloping. The tide pool, a critical part of the image, is especially soft.

For the final print (Figure 4), I used Brovira No. 5 paper, Amidol developer, and developed it for three minutes to keep the dull parts from going flat. As soon as you use high contrast papers, everything gets more critical. A second or two variation in exposure in high contrast areas can mean the difference between seeing what I want to see, and not seeing anything but black or white paper.

I could think of the negative-making process as one in which I would make a technically perfect negative. But the technically perfect negative doesn't always give me what I want. For instance, if a scene is very contrasty and you overexpose and underdevelop, you will compress the middle tones, which I don't want to do. I resort to extreme overexposure and underdevelopment if that is the only way to get any image at all. By not always reaching for the easily printed negative, I get luminosity I wouldn't otherwise have.

In the tide pool print, it's always been a touchy problem to get the brilliance in the pool itself, where the negative is soft. Unless carefully controlled, that part goes muddy. The rest of the photograph is secondary, but requires some burning and dodging to get tonal balance.

These are problems I've been living with. In doing so, I've developed printing skills. It's a way of life with me. In printing, I don't want to distort the reality of the image, but I don't want to distort the reality of my feelings for it either. The two go hand in hand. I have no qualms about altering the image by burning and dodging. I'm not a purist in that way. I am a purist in that I don't want the manipulation to show. As soon as it does, the magic is destroyed.

A perfect example of this is the print of the STARK TREE (Figure 5). I passed that place on a mountain freeway maybe a dozen times and never wanted to take a picture. But one day the clouds, the atmospheric feeling of the scene, appealed to me. I got out of my car, set up the 8 x 10 camera, and shot straight into the sun. I knew I was going to have a terrible problem with contrast, shooting into the sun with the deep shadow of the hill below it. I went ahead and photo-

AMIDOL PAPER DEVELOPER

water — ½ gallon
sodium sulfite — 3 tbsp.
amidol — 2 tsp
potassium bromide — 10cc
(10% solution)
BB solution (DuPont) — 10cc
citric acid — ½ tsp

Use full strength. Prints are fully developed in 40 seconds but can remain in this solution up to 6 minutes.

Figure 2.

graphed anyway, because it's something I felt. Later I suffered printing it, but this is a picture people always want.

I have to expose the bottom of the print enough to get some detail. It's so thin on the negative that it takes maybe eight seconds to expose, where the upper part takes up to two and a half minutes. Using Polycontrast paper with a No. 10 Varigam filter, I expose the bottom part. Then, as I burn in the sky, all the little trees on the hillside have to be carefully dodged or they disappear. (Though faint, they are absolutely essential to the mystery of the picture.) Then I start to burn in the sun. It is a tremendous problem because I want the sun to be a circle, but this requires so much light and time that the surrounding clouds go black. I keep working with smaller and smaller holes in my burning paper until I end up with just a tiny hole for the sun. Then the upper-right-hand corner must be balanced tonally with the left-hand corner. There has to be a unity of atmospheric tonality to create the effect I want. You can see what happens to the image if I print it straight for the bottom (Figure 6) or for the top (Figure 7). The prints, I believe, speak for themselves.

All my 8 x 10 negatives have to be printed on enlarging paper, which creates problems. The speed of these papers is much greater than that of the contact papers. This means I can't put enough light on certain key negatives to be able to see to dodge. But I've had to learn — the STARK TREE negative is very dense in the upper part. Where I exposed it for two minutes around the sun printing on a contact paper, with enlarging paper I expose it the same time, but must use a much weaker printing light. If I use enough light to see what I am doing when dodging, the clouds go black. With a weaker light I struggle to see the parts I wish to dodge.

About the same time that Convira was discontinued, Ansco stopped making Isopan, the film I used. I now use Plus-X or Panatomic-X roll film and the modified Stockler developer mentioned above.

You will notice in the prints that there are no large areas of deep black and almost no blocked highlights. These would threaten the symbolic role of the photograph for the viewer because deep blacks and blocked highlights have no substance from the standpoint of the photograph-as-symbol. For the viewer, the photograph-as-symbol is of primary importance. For the photographer, the thing that is symbolized is key. Being aware of this relationship helps develop one's visual and mental sensibilities. When one opens one's mind to the object symbolized, a new awareness develops in the picture-making process, a knowledge that direct perception is just surface awareness. It doesn't show the changing character of things, one of the deepest experiences we have. Everything in life and death is changing. Knowing this, one works out ways not only to record what one perceives, but by relating objects one evokes the quality of change.

The picture of the fallen redwood does this (Figure 8). The horsetails surrounding it have survived for fifty million years. They used to be as big as the redwoods are now. There is a visual relationship between the enduring horsetails and the dead redwood log that evokes a feeling of life and death. The redwood trunk will continue to become organic matter on which the horsetails and redwood seedlings feed and grow. The cyclical character of change is implicit in the image and finds its roots first in the thing symbolized and second in the photograph-as-symbol.

When photographing, I'm seldom aware of why I'm attracted to something. I intuit something I want. I am aware of constantly rejecting things. After I've photographed, I become aware of the ideas in the back of my head that caused me to make the picture. They were crystalized by looking at the objects to be photographed.

When you place things of the physical world together in a photograph to arouse feelings of change in the viewer, you add the dimension of time. The time faculty develops in the following way: you perceive things initially, later you perceive other things that influence the original perception, memories build, and your thoughts and feelings are altered by these memories. You can affect the picture by the relational qualities you give to the objects, and in so doing symbolize that deeply important element — change.

REDWOOD LOG AND HORSETAILS was made with 8 x 10 Isopan film. I printed it on Polycontrast enlarging paper with a No. 3 filter to obtain tonal brilliance. The horsetails are burned in, or dodged in different areas to achieve a greater sense of balanced luminosity. (Compare Figures 8 and 9.) When I print, I'm reacting to what I feel, what I want the print to say. I want it to look natural because it is of nature. (To me, people are also of nature.) Nature varies in its lights, but whatever the light, whether I modify it or not, I want it to look like natural light. It's completely legitimate and interesting to change the quality of light in a print, as long as it looks natural. The tonal balance of a picture is as important to me as the spatial balance of the masses.

The three prints of the CHILD IN THE FOREST show the progression toward a balanced final statement. Figure 10 was exposed for the forest, leaving the child's skin blocked and unnaturally white. In Figure 11, the exposure was made to print the child's skin with the proper tonal values. This made the forest go black. In the final print, Figure 12, both the child's skin values and the natural tones of the surrounding forest are balanced.

I've always had the feeling that there are certain laws of nature that govern us every minute of our lives. Gravity is one of them. How do we live with it? One way is to learn to balance. If you see something that looks like it's going to fall, this makes you uncomfortable. Well, it's the same with a picture. If you have a picture that makes you feel there is too much tonal and/or mass emphasis on one side, it makes you uncomfortable. Some people disregard this sense of balance because they're thinking of other things: for instance, when they take a social or political picture of a fellow hitting someone with a club, they care about the event to the exclusion of everything else. In many documentary pictures this concern is unavoidable, but the fact remains that balance is an integral part of our life experience. I like to have a picture balanced; there's a kind of peace when you feel everything working together. It's also exciting because it is a challenge to be able to perceive and create balance in a photograph. Of course, I don't mean to imply that all photographs have to be balanced. The subject matter determines whether balance or imbalance is needed.

I'm sure you've had the experience of making a print that feels right. Well, to get a second one like it can be a big problem. Some steps in the first print require split-second timing, especially the dodging. Being able to repeat a good print is the kind of technical expertise learned only by attention to processing details and constant "eye" training. I rate the development of a fine technique as 25 percent book and instructional training and 75 percent "eye" training.

In the popular magazines I see photographs by some of the best technicians in the world, but these are usually the worst pictures I've ever seen because they have little sense of tone or balance. Tone, balance, and other visual senses are all part of "eye" training. If one has a keen sense of what is needed in a picture, one has to know how to get it. But if you know a lot of technique and don't have a sense of direction, the technique is useless. Picture sense only comes with the development of one's own faculties. Except to a limited degree, it can't be learned from books or teachers. Nature, from whence all things come, cannot be packaged in neat little academic boxes to be opened as needed.

Space, time, opposites, reality, existence, ordering, and the thing ordered have become principle-theories, which I have come to believe in through my years of work. They have become supportive, not alone to my photography, but to my life in general. They developed from my contacts with nature and have been later substantiated by reading the writings of great philosophers and scientists. I have subjected them to endless visual tests only to find their meaning enhanced. They are tools of thought that have permitted me to grow visually and to have the foundation for a way of life.

FILM	ASA RATING	DEVELOPER	SOLUTION & TIME	AGITATION
Plus-X ——— Panatomic-X	Normal	Modified Stockler formula ——— 70 F	Solution A: metol— 10 grams sodium sulfite — 150 grams water — 2000cc ——— Solution B: borax — 20 grams water — 2000cc ——— 4½ minutes	8x10: Nitrogen burst ——— Roll film: raise and lower reel slowly, ¼ inch movements in container of developer

ENLARGER	LENS	LIGHT SOURCE	USUAL APERTURE	USUAL EXPOSURE
Omega D2 ——— CB-7	Schneider Componon 100mm *f*/5.6 ——— Schneider Componon 150mm *f*/5.6	Point light source	Varied	Varied

PAPER	DEVELOPER	SOLUTION & TIME	STOP BATH	FIXER
Polycontrast F ——— Brovira III Nos. 5 and 6	Amidol	Amidol: full strength ——— water — ½ gallon sodium sulfite — 3 tbsp amidol — 2 tsp potassium bromide, 10% solution* — 10cc BB solution — 10cc citric acid — ½ tsp ——— 40 seconds to 6 minutes	Kodak Indicator ——— 20 seconds	GAF Acid fix solution ——— 2 baths ——— 3½ minutes in each

WASH	TONING	DRYING	FLATTENING	PRESENTATION
5 minutes hypo eliminator ——— 1 hour in archival washer	Selenium ——— Per instructions ——— 20 seconds to 6 minutes in solution of selenium and hypo clearing agent**	Air dry on fiberglass screen	Prints are drymounted	Under glass

*10% solution: Dissolve 10 grams in 90cc water, add sufficient water to make 100cc.

**4 ounces selenium, 3 ounces Perma Wash, 1 gallon of water at 68 F

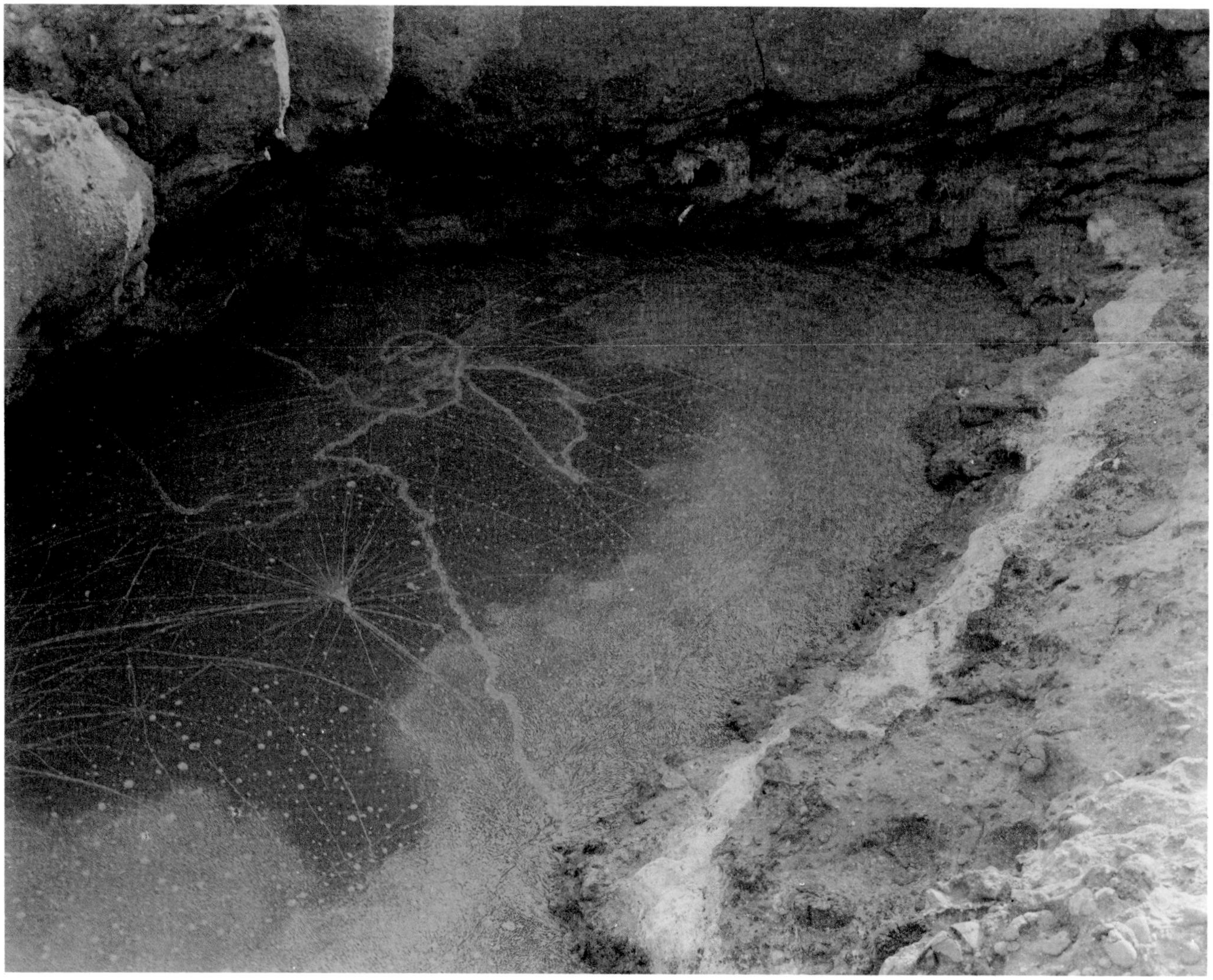

Figure 3: POINT LOBOS TIDE POOL (printed from soft negative)

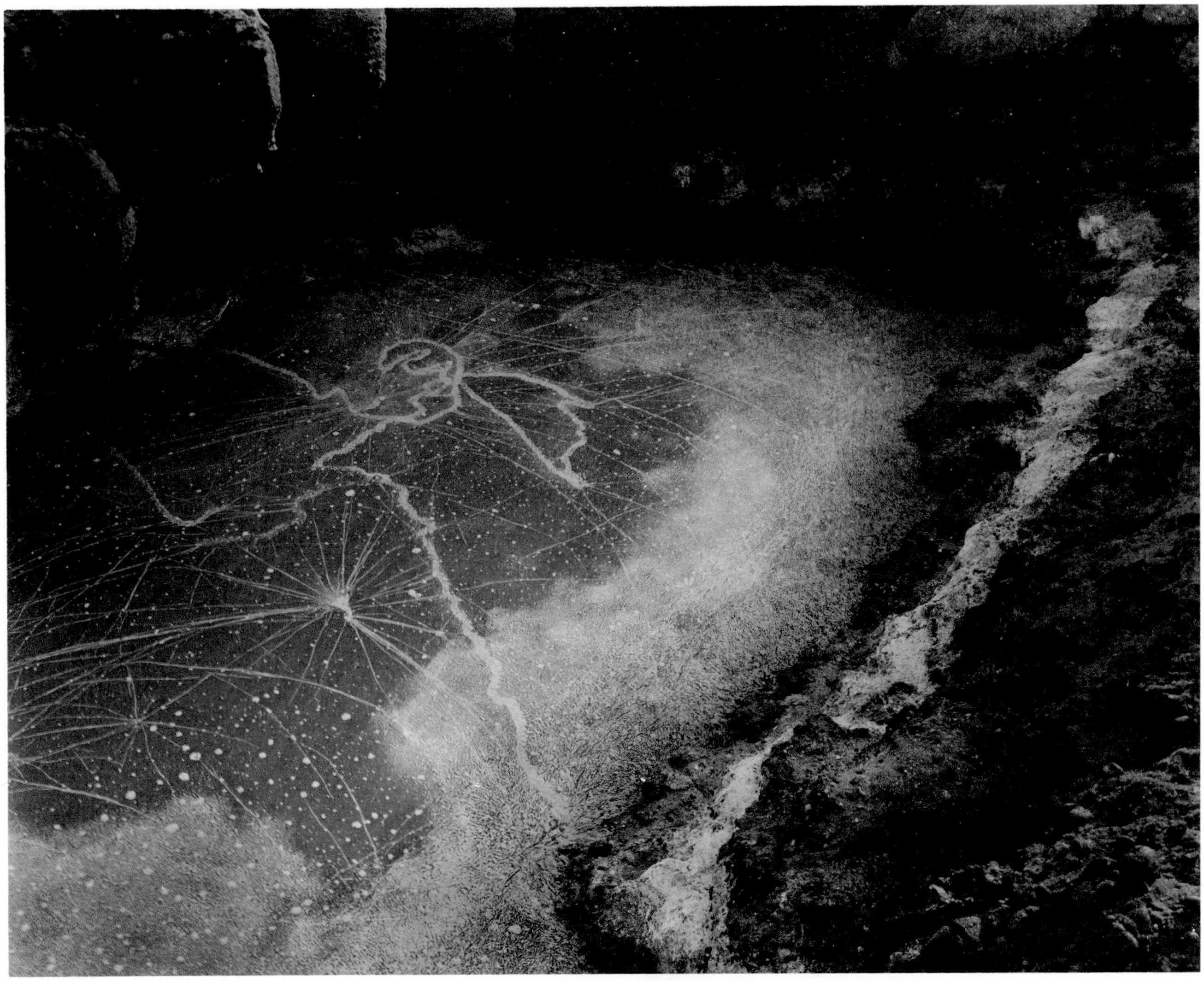

Figure 4: POINT LOBOS TIDE POOL (final print)

Figure 5: STARK TREE (final print)

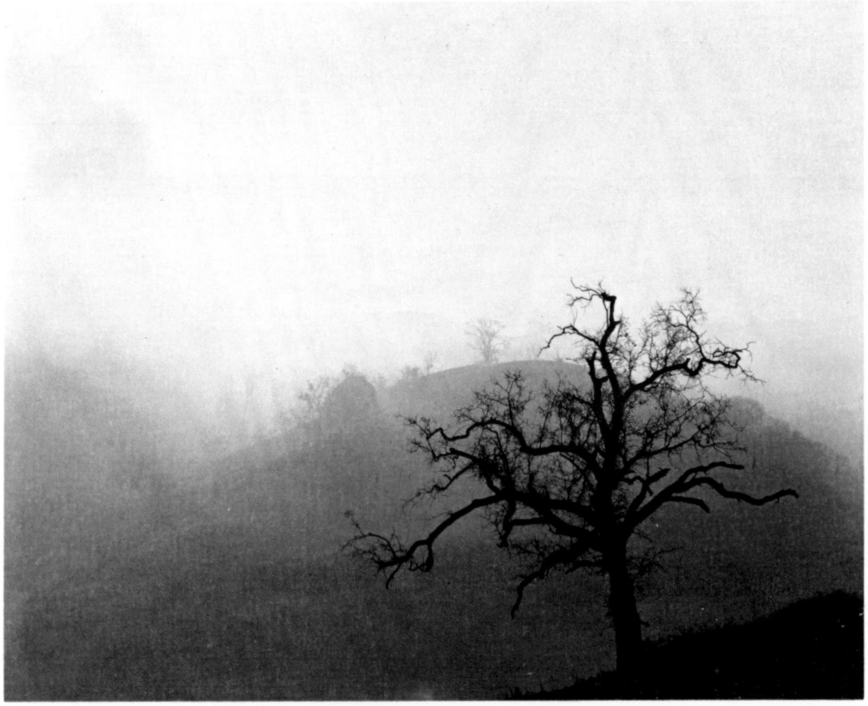

Figure 6: STARK TREE (printed for bottom area)

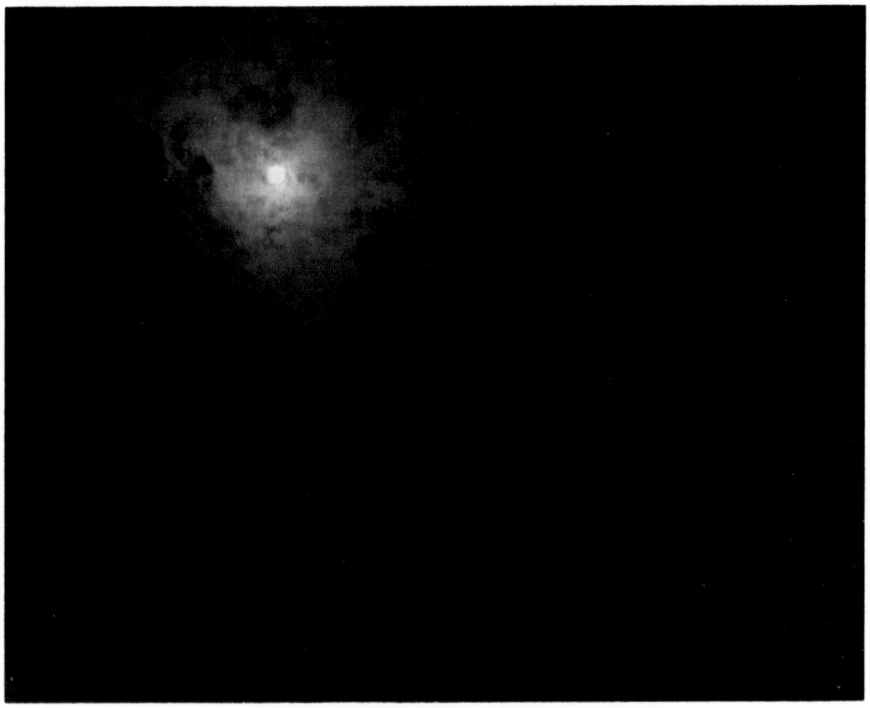

Figure 7: STARK TREE (printed for top area)

Figure 8: REDWOOD LOG AND HORSETAILS (final print)

Figure 9: REDWOOD LOG AND HORSETAILS (before dodging and burning)

Figure 10: CHILD IN THE FOREST (exposed for forest)

Figure 11: CHILD IN THE FOREST (exposed for skin tones)

Figure 12: CHILD IN THE FOREST (final print)

JERRY BURCHARD

Jerry Burchard was born in Rochester, New York, in 1931, a third generation Kodak worker. In 1952, he joined the Navy and attended photography school, finishing his service as a photography mate stationed in Italy.

In 1956, he enrolled in the California School of Fine Arts, which later became the San Francisco Art Institute. On graduation, he freelanced both in San Francisco and New York City until 1966 when he returned to teach at the San Francisco Art Institute. He later became Chairman of the Photography Department there.

In 1976 Burchard received a National Endowment for the Arts grant and is currently on sabbatical from the San Francisco Art Institute.

Selected one-man shows:

1975: Texas Gallery, Houston, Texas
American Gallery, San Francisco

1976: Center of the Eye, Sun Valley, Idaho

Selected collections:
George Eastman House, Rochester, New York
Pasadena Museum of Art, Pasadena, California
Visual Studies Workshop, Rochester, New York
Fogg Art Museum, Cambridge, Massachusetts
Houston Museum of Fine Art, Houston, Texas
Seattle Museum of Art, Seattle, Washington

Don Long

I've always been interested in walking around with a camera in the evening. I started doing it almost as soon as I began taking pictures. I was twelve when I took my first picture. It was of some teddy bears in a cherry tree. That night I came back and tried a time exposure which didn't come out. The next time I remember photographing at night was in Italy while in the Navy. One day I borrowed a 35mm Kodak Retina and went out and shot a one-ring circus in Naples. I never printed those negatives because they were shaky and full of weird lights and stuff, and besides, they looked so small — not like a 4 x 5 or 8 x 10. Fifteen years later, after I got into night photography, I rediscovered those negatives. They were what I had been trying to do for years but who could have accepted those images in the fifties?

One night I was visiting friends in a San Francisco high-rise. We were all watching TV, getting drunk and loaded, and I was shooting down from their balcony. I just felt like something was happening, and on the way home that night I stopped in an alley and shot off half a roll, leaning against cars and buildings and walls. Coming through Washington Square Park, it was overcast and there was a nice set of grays, so I shot off the rest of the roll. I took my first picture in the park, standing for thirty seconds on one foot for a Zen joke. But the joke was on me because the picture was rock steady, and I knew I was hooked for life. What appealed to me more and more was that my camera was seeing things I couldn't, day or night. You just let it go—thirty seconds, five minutes, forty minutes. We all know that what our eyes can see is limited, especially at night, but if you allow the camera to overexpose enough, it starts discovering new levels of gray and new planes. Some things get so overexposed that they turn into new objects. I have a picture of the stars from Morocco. It was taken in Agadir, a town notorious for earthquakes. My camera was leaning on a solid concrete stairway for five minutes. But when I developed the negative, there was just a little bit of a shake in the star trails, probably from one of the tremors. That little extra hook in the stars makes the picture vibrate.

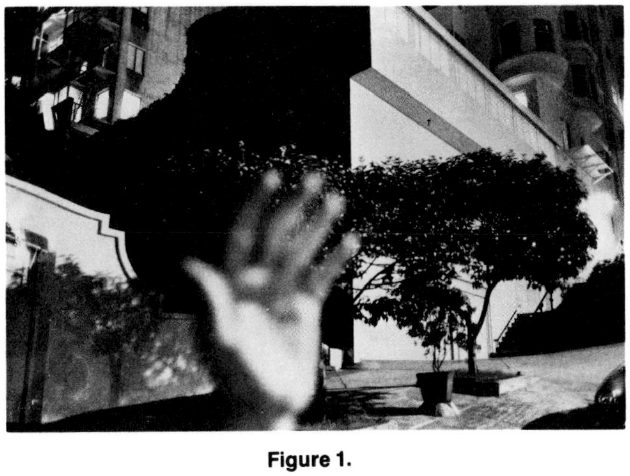

Figure 1.

To determine my exposure, I just throw my finger in the air to see which way the exposure is blowing (Figure 1). I take a look at my hand and I know by the value on my palm how long the exposure will be. If it's going to be a five or fifteen minute exposure, then I just have to guess. I've had to estimate forty minute exposures and hour exposures as well. One night while I was living in Spain, outside a little village, there was a fiesta. So I put the camera on a high post and went into town, had a couple of drinks, and came back about an hour later and took the camera down. I thought about it some more, put the camera back up, and went into town again for a forty-five minute drink. As it turned out, the hour exposure worked better. It was a low key profile of the village, and right at the bottom were some trees and things, with all the stars streaked in a curve across the sky. Now I can look at the star streaks in my photographs and know intuitively how long the exposure was.

I'm not trying to sound mysterious, but when I leave the house I know whether I should take my camera with me or not. If I feel I should and don't, I'll inevitably curse myself later. I trust those instincts. When I get to a location, something hits me, like divining for water. I feel hot. Then I hold my breath and the exposure just comes on. I feel like I'm being lit up, definitely getting off.

For me, the camera is as much a partner in the action as myself or the object to be photographed, and this seems to prove itself over and over again. A given camera will regulate your philosophy on how and what to photograph. With a beautiful but awkward piece of equipment, like a Hasselblad, you're not going to photograph something you might use a half-frame for. My Hasselblad helped me through most of my early travails and led me to a peak. Then, after fifteen years, a half frame Olympus Pen W liberated me in six months from every bit of that formal 2¼ vision. So I lean on my machine. I don't even look. I just let my fingers and the machine decide what's going to be manipulated. My decision is what to point it at and what the exposure will be. The camera sees more than I can, so I give it plenty of rope and watch what happens. The look of my pictures should show this somehow. For instance, if you look at pictures taken on acid or peyote or dope or wine, you can see these influences in every one of the pictures. The work of writers like Poe and Baudelaire shows that they used a lot of opium. What's interesting to me in art is the revelation of new worlds. Otherwise, why bother?

For ten years I've been using the same lens and the same camera for my night work. I've never used a fifty on my Nikon SP. I've had other cameras on and off in that time, but always the same 35mm on that body. It helps a lot, when you're in the dark, to know even without looking through the viewfinder, what you're going to get in the picture. Eventually, your eyes get accustomed to seeing in terms of your equipment and material. You can look at a scene, place an invisible square or rectangle around it and know exactly what's going to be in the frame and what's not. When you look at something, you anticipate the picture. It becomes automatic, like shifting gears in a car.

I always shoot at *f*/2.8. Although it's an *f*/2.5 lens, I stop down for that minimal possibility of getting something in better focus. Once I started doing this, I just kept it up. It didn't cost me a thing. All the photographers I've ever met have lived perhaps too much by technical superstition.

I switched to Tri-X a long time ago for convenience. I've used other films, but it's the only one you can buy in any store, anytime, any place.

I expose my film at ASA 200 and develop it in FG-7, for twelve minutes at 70 F using four ounces to sixty-four ounces of water. That's about a one to sixteen solution. Agitation is the thing that's really serious. My favorite agitation of all time belonged to a guy I went to school with, Akio Okumoto. His method was to take a two-reel can with Plus-X in it and whatever developer he was using, shake it and turn it upside down. Halfway through the development, he'd put it right side up. That would be it until he opened the can to put in the hypo. One agitation, and the film came out perfect every time. I brooded about that, as you can imagine, for years. Then there's Blair Stapp's method. First of all, Blair is very tall and built his sink four feet high. Second, he had cans that would hold nine reels of 120mm; that's equivalent to eighteen rolls of 35mm, if you really want to go berserk. Using his darkroom, I had to stand on a stool to get to the top of the can to pour in the developer. In the dark, of course. Then, as he taught me, I'd put the tank on the floor of the sink and roll it back and forth briskly, really outrageously, so the reels spun around inside. It was like a hot rod track, those little reels going yoing-yoing-yoing. For my agitation, I combine all of these moves: I give the can the old milk-shake toss for ten seconds out of every minute, just like they recommend; about every third move I roll it and spin the reels, or just rest the tank upside down. All of this at a one to sixteen ratio instead of a one to fifteen, and I come out with perfect film every time. This is with an eight-roll can which a lot of people suspect doesn't really work, but it's very efficient. It's got to be all superstition, right? I just used everyone's method that I came across. What else have you got to do for twelve minutes . . . just go nuts?

When I smoked, I always left the darkroom for a cigarette about seven minutes through the development. When I stopped smoking, my film stopped coming out right. I finally remembered the break. So now about seven minutes through the development, I take a break and return after a minute and a half, and my film is coming out perfect again. Although I've talked a lot about technique, I try to keep mine as simple as possible. If something's really going to be difficult to print, then I don't want to use that negative. It's something I picked up from using the I-Tek machine. An I-Tek machine is a desk console with a vertical screen for 35mm microfilm that prints a dry copy in twenty seconds. In four hours, four weeks of darkroom work can be accomplished. I think of I-Teks as proofs rather than finished prints, but I use them for special shows and also for personal shots for friends (weddings, souvenirs, etc.). It has finally relieved me of the guilt photographers suffer for unprinted negatives. Some negatives were impossible to use on the machine. Some negatives are worth going through a little trouble for, but I would rather be able to lay 'em down on No. 2 paper without burning or dodging and develop them for exactly a minute and a half, whether I do ten or twenty of them. That way, when I have to reprint, it's easier.

Although I think Agfa puts out the finest paper, I've had to print some negatives over and over again, switching from Portriga No. 2 to No. 3 paper because their emulsions change. They must leave out a little silver each year. Paper doesn't get any better, for sure, but I wouldn't hit a dog in the ass with the other companies' papers. There's just not enough silver in any of them.

I started on Brovira and now use Portriga, which is limited. It doesn't have all the contrasts, but it's okay. Again, if I can't print it on Nos. 2, 3 or 4, then I just don't use it.

When I get into the darkroom, it takes me an hour to work into the rhythm, and after that I don't think about any of the details. They take care of themselves. For instance, each day I pick a time on the second hand to immerse the paper in the developer. For the rest of the day the paper comes out of the easel coordinated to match that time without my even looking. I feel very Zen about the whole thing, because it just works out that way.

First of all, I work in a darkroom that's quite big. it has a large sink, and I use large trays, 20 x 24 or larger. The first tray contains Edwal TST, a developer concentrate mixed one to ten at 70 F. TST one to seven is as strong as straight Dektol. At one to seven you can take a No. 6 paper and jam it to a No. 8. You can almost see the smoke come out, it's that strong. TST has another advantage besides utterly variable contrast possibilities. If it's an inch deep, it'll last a week without oxidizing. You don't even have to cover it.

The next tray contains a strong solution of short-stop, something I learned from making umpteen copies in the Navy. I don't measure the glacial acetic acid: you know, glug-glug-glug-glug. I put the print in the short-stop and it sizzles. A piece of paper goes in and I turn it four times; in other words, I spend thirty seconds in the short-stop.

So, first a minute and a half in the developer, then thirty seconds in the short-stop. The third tray contains standard hypo mixed from a liquid concentrate. Both the short-stop and the hypo trays hold about four gallons each. The developer is three gallons and the hypo-eliminator is four. I mix deep solutions to allow for multiple printings.

Next comes a quick water bath and then hypo-eliminator, then another water bath in one of those rocking washers that tilt back and forth, for about half an hour. I dry and selenium tone the prints another day. For reducing I put them dry into Ansel Adams' Quick Bleach for thirty seconds:

ANSEL ADAMS' QUICK BLEACH THE PRINT, BASIC PHOTO 3 Copyright 1950, by Ansel Adams. Reprinted by permission of New York Graphic Society.
Solution A: water — 300cc potassium ferricyanide — 62.5 grams potassium metabisulfite or sodium bisulfite — 4.2 grams water to make 500cc
Solution B: ammonium thiocyanate — 330 grams potassium bromide — 30 grams water to make 1000cc
Mix 1 part Solution A with 2 parts Solution B and add to 15 parts water. Immerse print face up, agitate vigorously for 5 to 10 seconds. Transfer to tray of water and agitate until bleaching solution is assumed to have been removed. Return to bath if necessary, for a few seconds only. It is advisable to work with dry prints.

This solution bleaches the middle gray tones and cleans up the image. Then into another water bath, followed by the selenium toner, one part selenium to nine parts water, for three to five minutes. With that strength solution, six and a half minutes will turn a print red, I mean really red. But in five minutes, you can barely see the red creeping in. I like a little of the red. (Portriga's already slightly reddish brown.) Then, water, hypo-eliminator and final wash. I try to print just a bit on the gray side and then use selenium to snap up the blacks and give the illusion of whitening the whites. Portriga adds another tint that, with selenium and TST, gets me the color I'm after. I prefer to dry the prints on a drum dryer, but occasionally air dry and then flatten in a mounting press. We've discussed about twelve different solutions for each print, which makes it pretty hard to get a good count out of your work. I lose about thirty percent.

My darkroom set-up includes two Leitz enlargers, two 16 x 20 easels, a couple of timers, and God, boxes and boxes of paper. I use a 250 watt bulb, No. 213 in the enlarger, to cut down on exposure time. This way my exposures are usually about fifteen seconds to a minute. Before, they were all a minute, five minutes, fifteen minutes. It was driving me nuts. Although there's plenty to complain about with the Leitz, it does hold the negative in a flat plane so it won't buckle. When I was printing larger format negatives in other enlargers, and using a bright bulb, I'd have to leave the lamp on all the time; otherwise, every time the negative cooled down, it would buckle from where I had focused it.

Leitz enlargers are not really meant for 16 x 20 prints. If you raise them high enough to print that size and let loose at the wing nut, they'll drop right on your head. Also, the auto-focus mechanism does nothing except get in the way and immediately breaks. Worst of all, you have to file out your own negative carrier, if you want to print the full negative.

Using two enlargers, or sometimes three, literally cuts the time in half or in thirds. I set up the negatives and start testing, chopping 16 x 20 paper into 5 x 7 pieces. I estimate the exposure, depending on how thick the negative looks, and start them off at *f*/8, with fifteen second intervals —fifteen, thirty, forty-five, a minute—doing these test strips for both negatives at once. When I feel I can reckon an exposure, I do another test strip on that exposure for each negative. By this time I've been in the dark for quite a while, with no pictures yet. Finally, I reach the rough exposure for each negative and make the first prints. Then I look at both of them and if there's any burning or dodging or contrast change needed, I try one more print. When I know what I'm going to do with each negative, I go into production, doing five, ten, or however many I'm going to print of each. I use both enlargers at once and keep the prints in an empty box.

Yesterday, I was doing the RAINBOW picture (Figure 5); and the MOROCCAN TEAHOUSE (Figure 6). The RAINBOW was a forty-five second exposure, and the TEAHOUSE was only ten seconds, but needed a little burning on the top. So while I was exposing the forty-five second RAINBOW, I was able to do both exposures on the TEAHOUSE. I did fifteen each of those two negatives. When they were finished, I took the box and fanned the prints out in two directions (Figure 2) and then, just like I had 8 x 10's or postcards, I'd wham 'em into the developer (Figure 3), checking the clock to make sure how long it took to get them in, rotating and shuffling them back and forth. I took them out of the developer one at a time (Figure 4), again in the same order and at the same rate that they went in. Then I put them all in a short-stop, one by one, and circulated them. When you have that many pieces of paper, you shuffle them back and forth like decks of cards. They float all over the water that way. (I used to do maybe a hundred 8 x 10 prints at a time when I was in the Navy.) Then I picked them up all at once and let them drain, and put them into the hypo, rotating them fast. I agitated continually for a couple of minutes. You've got to, otherwise you get all kinds of stains. If I have a lot of this production work, my assistant, Tazio Moriya, usually comes in to help. An extra hand in a sink full of 16 x 20's is always useful.

Phil Perkis taught me how to print 35mm while we were working at a lab in New York. There was so much produc-

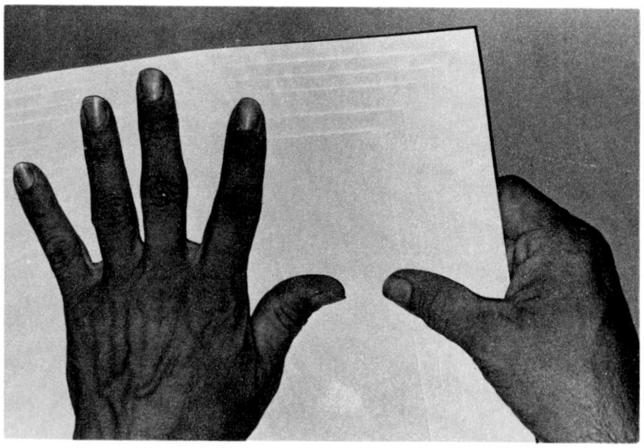

Figure 2.

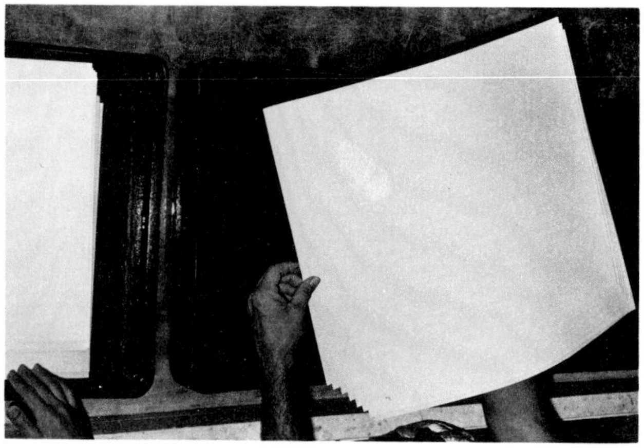

Figure 3.

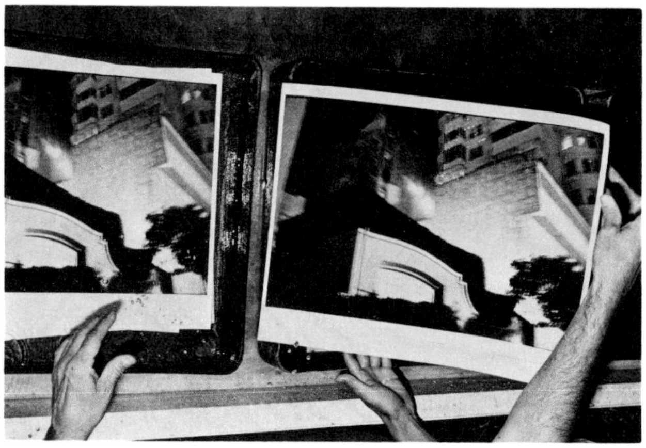

Figure 4.

tion, and the quality they asked for was so low, that I learned from Phil how to look at a negative in the enlarger, give it the estimated exposure, and put the thing in a box. When I had printed twenty-five sheets of paper that way, I threw them in the developer and pulled them out at random. It taught me how to print from 35mm negatives and it also got me into heavy, serious production. I like the idea of doing production. For one thing, you're not so bored. I hate the darkroom so bad that I do each step as perfectly as I can. Otherwise, I'm wasting my time for the rest of the process. I know some people who are happy as bugs in the darkroom, but I think it stinks. I don't like the way I smell, it smells, or anything else about it. It's real drudgery. If I have to go in there, I want to get the best product I can with the least amount of effort. But I also found out that being too persnickety in any part of the process only leads you to bad conclusions. I like to keep everything simple, so all my concentration can be on the quality of the print.

One time I copped to Imogen Cunningham how much I hated the darkroom and all the details that went with it. I thought she'd be one of those darkroom lovers. I told her that people come up to me and say, "Oh, don't you just love working in the darkroom?" and all that crap. Then I asked her, "What do you tell them?" and she said, "I tell them they should try it for sixty years."

When I shot FORTY MINUTES IN NOVATO (Figure 7), I was on some kind of South American psychedelic trip, and it was about three in the morning. I looked out the back porch, a little balcony, and it was pitch black. I could hardly see my hand, and down there in the valley I could just barely make out a weird forest. I set my camera on the railing and took four exposures, ranging from thirty seconds to forty minutes. I literally wet my finger and waved it up in the air and came down with forty minutes. What else are you going to do when it's pitch black? I didn't even know the mountains existed at the time. The weather was overcast, so it looks like a foggy afternoon but it's a forty minute exposure of pitch black. No moon. No sun. No city lights. This is in the sticks. In front, all the bushes are white because inside the house, about fifty feet behind a glass wall, there was a small red votive candle. In forty minutes it wiped out the bushes, almost took the texture out of them.

Both winter pictures were taken at Christmas time in New England, but in different years. They are like brothers. The sky was overcast and there was a lot of snow when I took the Rochester picture (Figure 10) All those bright lights in the background aren't only street lights. There are outdoor Christmas tree lights, too. In fifteen seconds the colored lights burned out to a dead white. I pushed the camera up against the window pane and exposed for fifteen seconds as the camera slid down the glass. Same thing with the second picture. I was staying overnight with Elaine Mayes and Bill Arnold in Florence, Massachusetts, and I saw this great scene going on outside their house (Figure 9), so I put the camera up against the glass and slid down for fifteen seconds. The strange light on the right hand side of the picture is that peculiar kind of streaking that street lights produce on cold nights on the East Coast. Maybe it's a different kind of bulb from out here in California, maybe it's the cold, but you don't get that in the West. This looks a little like a Hallmark card, but I hope it is spooky enough so it would never be taken for one.

The MOROCCAN VILLAGE (Figure 8) was taken in Goulimine, right on the edge of the Sahara Desert. What you see in the foreground are the ruins of an old fortress. I've got my camera jammed into a crevice somewhere in a wall. (I never have used a tripod.) Once I got the camera comfortable and me comfortable, I just sat down and counted off "one thousand one's" until I got to fifteen minutes. That was my exposure estimate for this, and as it turned out, not far off. Moroccan towns are lit mostly by candle or kerosene lamp. All this is kerosene lamplight. The only other light is moonlight. And, of course, behind the hills on the horizon just below the star streaks, you see a faint light, just a little bit of dawn coming from around the other side of the world.

I don't usually have light sources in my pictures. This is an exception. I had no choice. To the naked eye, most of these buildings weren't lit brightly, but just looking at even a small kerosene or gas lamp for fifteen minutes is going to make it seem pretty bright. I try to keep street lights out of most of my pictures because they annoy me terribly.

I hate burning and dodging; but I dodged out the foreground in this print just a speck, and burned the sky in a bit. I lose a lot of stars doing this, but otherwise the eye tends to slip out of the picture because everything else is so dark. It's nothing but a pile of blacks with a couple of whites.

There is this block known for its bushes in San Francisco. It is the hottest bush neighborhood in town. I know a lady who photographs hedges exclusively, and she turned me on to this block as a personal favor. I used to visit the block often to photograph a clump across from this garage. I never got anything good; so in desperation I turned around and photographed the garage (Figure 11) about four shots—around thirty seconds each. Months later, while watching the TV show "McMillan and Wife," the nagging suspicion that I was suffering from bush déjà-vu hit me as the camera swept past those treelets and followed the McMillan's limo into their driveway. Today, I still visit these bushes, a lost love. I had to settle for a garage.

To get the RAINBOW picture (Figure 5), I went to a park in

Casablanca, two blocks from my hotel, at about twelve every night. It was winter and really chilly. I'd sit and freeze every time I went there, but I was unable to expose a picture for almost two months. I traveled out of Casablanca a lot, and as soon as I got back I'd always go to the park. Weird incidents happened to me and I had a great time, but never took any pictures. Then, a few nights before I left Morocco, I went down there and I just knew it was the right time. I squeezed off quite a few, shooting from all the positions I had tried before. This picture was taken leaning back into a pile of bushes and hand holding the camera for thirty seconds. I shot two pictures, with one *f*-stop difference. They're identical otherwise, except one has a rainbow in it. I have lots of streaks going through my pictures all the time, little dots and dashes and alternating current. It doesn't get less mysterious for me, even when I know what they are. This time I feel I got that rainbow because I deserved it.

I try to have a print come out looking as if I'm not too fussy. I don't mount my pictures any more. I mean them to be seen exactly as they are, so you can see the writing on them with the signature and the white borders. They should be flattened out and put behind plastic instead of glass because the green of the glass cancels out too much of the mellow warm color of the toned Portriga. When I put so much work into a print, watching it turn from Portriga back to Brovira behind glass is a heartbreaker.

For the last two years, I've been working with twenty or thirty negatives, and it is strange. Most people do fifty or a hundred things a year. Some of them will work, and some won't. I've decided to limit myself in this way. It's killing me, too, because I hate to print the same things over and over again, but each time I print them, they do get better.

Like all the other people in the sixties, I used a lot of super-wide angle lenses and printed everything on No. 6. Bang! Since then, I've mellowed out a lot. As I print things over and over, they usually go to a lower contrast. The I-Tek machine taught me a lot about printing. It's got so many gray tones and no really solid black. My eyes developed a liking for grays, I guess, and I began seeing in those terms.

Since I shoot instinctively I don't mind if things are a little shaky or if there are blurs or things out of focus. If the picture is holding itself together, then these things are expressing time/life for me. I can look at a picture, and what I remember is not just me standing there at that corner, but what I remember is getting high while I was taking the picture. If you kiss someone who's really beautiful, you get off, and the same thing is true when you take a picture. You should feel as if you're glowing. Sometimes I could swear I was overexposing my own picture just from standing there. I hope that those feelings come through (Figure 12).

FILM	ASA RATING	DEVELOPER	SOLUTION & TIME	AGITATION
Tri-X	200	FG-7 ——— 70F	1:16 ——— 12 minutes	5 seconds in every 30 seconds ——— Roll, inversion, flat bottom combination

ENLARGER	LENS	LIGHT SOURCE	USUAL APERTURE	USUAL EXPOSURE
Focomat 1C	EL-Nikkor 50mm *f*/2.8	No. 213	*f*/8	Varied

PAPER	DEVELOPER	SOLUTION & TIME	STOP BATH	FIXER
Portriga III Nos. 2 to 4	TST	1:10 ——— 1½ minutes	Small amount of 100% glacial acetic acid added directly to water tray ——— 30 seconds	Kodak F-7 ——— One bath ——— 5 to 10 minutes

WASH	TONING	DRYING	FLATTENING	PRESENTATION
5 minutes running water ——— 5 minutes hypo eliminator ——— 30 minutes in rocking washer	Selenium ——— 1:9 ——— 3 to 5 minutes	Drum dryer	Sandwiched between museum boards, under weights or in drymount press	Unmounted ——— Prefers plexiglas

Figure 5: RAINBOW

Figure 6: MOROCCAN TEA HOUSE

Figure 7: FORTY MINUTES IN NOVATO

Figure 8: MOROCCAN VILLAGE

Figure 9: CHRISTMAS IN FLORENCE

Figure 10: CHRISTMAS IN ROCHESTER

Figure 11: GARAGE

Figure 12.

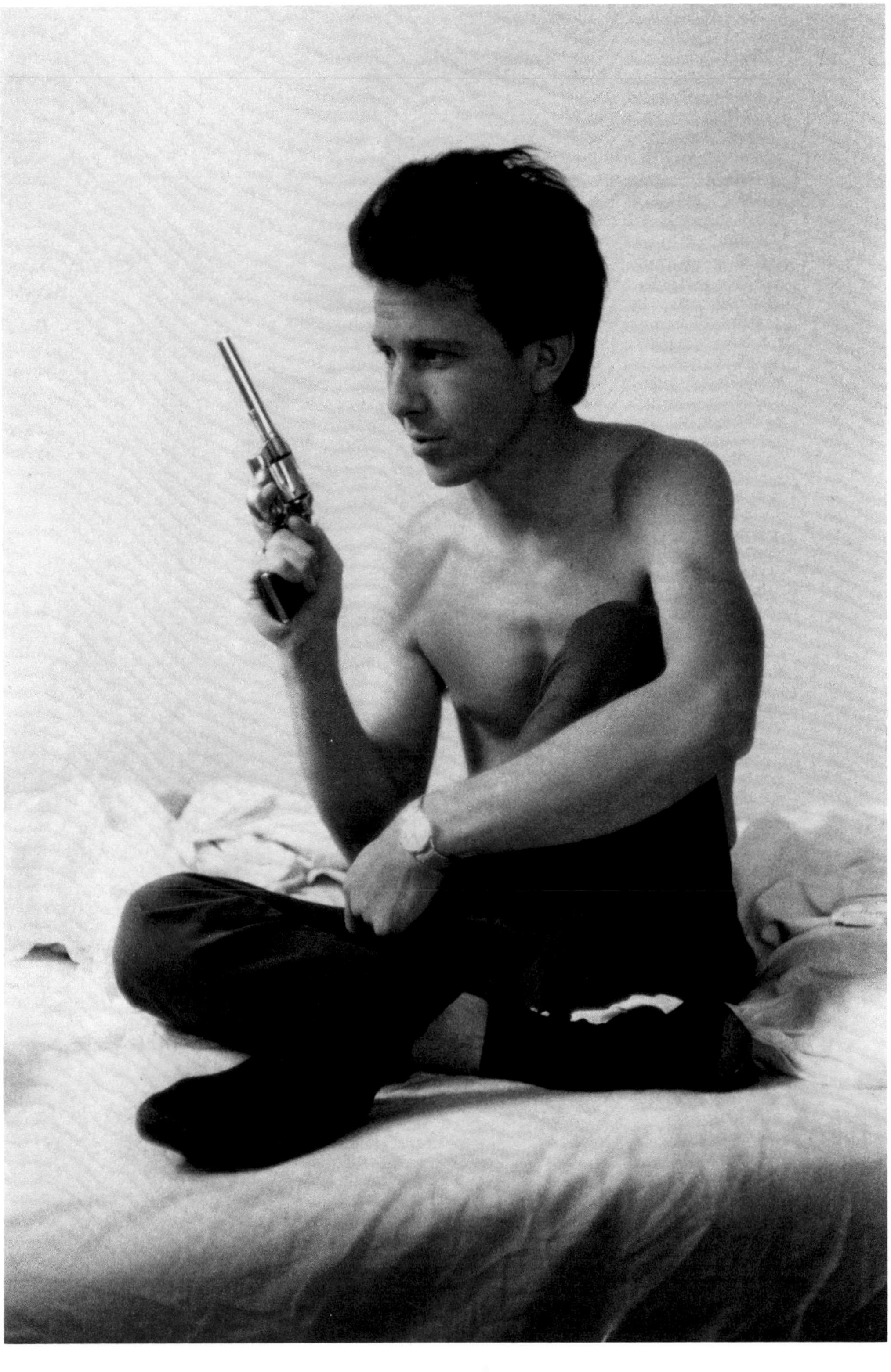

LARRY CLARK

Larry Clark was born in Tulsa, Oklahoma, in 1943. At sixteen, he entered the family commercial portraiture business, taking baby pictures himself.

On graduating from high school in 1961, he went to Milwaukee to attend the Layton School of Art, where he majored in photography and later became assistant to the photographer Walter Sheffer.

In 1964 he moved to New York City to freelance but was drafted within two months and sent to Vietnam.

Once out of the Army, he returned to Tulsa and began to photograph again. He has traveled extensively around the United States and Mexico.

By 1970 he was back in Tulsa, and in 1971 his book TULSA (Lustrum Press, New York) was published. He received a National Endowment for the Arts grant in 1973.

Selected one-man shows:

1972: University of North Dakota Art Gallery, Grand Forks

1973: New York State University, Buffalo
Western Carolina University, Cullowhee, North Carolina

1974: Oakton College, Martin Grove, Illinois

1975: Kirkland College, Clinton, New York

1976: New England School of Photography, Boston

1977: Photography Gallery Society, Saskatoon, Canada

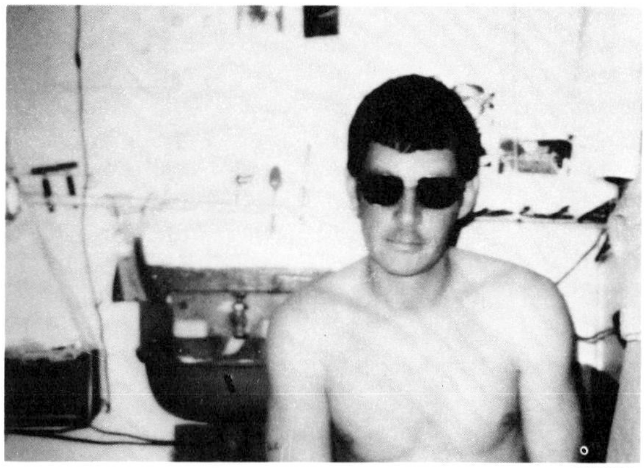

93353

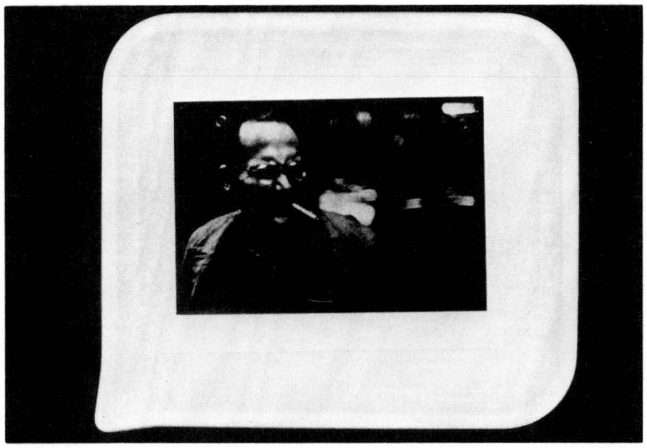

Figure 1A

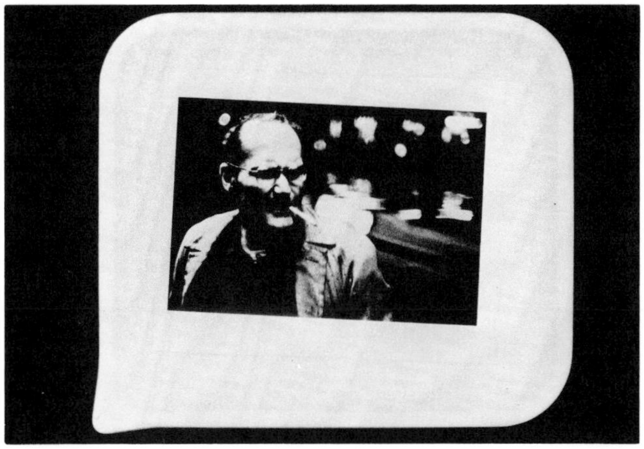

Figure 1B

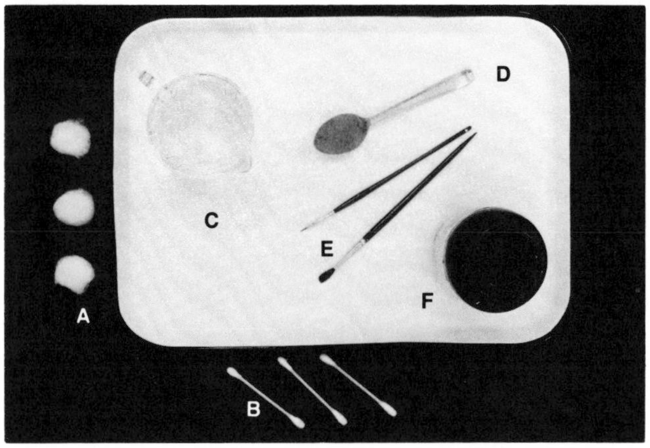

Figure 2.
A: Cotton balls B: Q-tips C: Water D: Teaspoon
E: Sable brushes F: Ferricyanide solution

i guess the first time i used ferricyanide was back at school. i'd made about thirty prints and after drying them, found they were dark and gray. muddy highlights. then an old newspaper photographer who was teaching that day told me i could save them by soaking them for five or ten minutes in a very weak bleach bath. i filled a big tray with water, added just a tad of the yellow powder, and soaked the prints (Figure 1A). after a few minutes i threw them in the hypo and watched them snap (Figure 1B). you usually can't see the ferricyanide work until you put the print back in the hypo, which you have to do to stop and kill the bleach. the bleach appears to attack the highlights faster than the shadow, so when i threw the print in the hypo all the highlights snapped on. the prints looked better. another student in the darkroom was printing an out-of-focus picture and told the teacher he couldn't get it in focus. the teacher reached in a cabinet and got a little bottle of liquid he called in-focus developer. the guy made another print using the in-focus developer and thought it was sharper. ferricyanide seemed to work, too.

i started working for a good photographer in milwaukee, water sheffer. he was into photo chemistry and taught me. we mixed all the chemicals from scratch and he'd explain what each ingredient did. here's an old defender paper developer formula that we used and i still do. the great thing about this developer is you get much richer blacks than you can get from dektol. mixing your own chemicals is cheap. if you have to use dektol, mix it one to one and throw some bromide in the tray for the blacks. this developer is great for polycontrast paper:

elon — ½ oz. sodium sulfite — 10 oz. hydraquinone — 2¾ oz. sodium carbonite — 20 oz. potassium bromide — 96 grains or ¼ oz.
mix in one gallon of water at 125 F. this is the ultimate blue-black paper developer. use straight or 1:1.

i was looking at w. eugene smith's work a lot and studying how he printed and all the ferricyanide he used. i tried to print like him. i would go in the darkroom for weeks and not come out. printing deep and rich and then bringing out the highlights and opening shadows with bleach. i use a weak solution (a teaspoon of potassium ferricyanide to a cup of water) and work on sections of the print with a brush or cotton swab (Figure 2). then into the hypo to see what's happened. here's a print from that period of gene smith, whom i met on the street one night in new york city (Figure 3). it's got ferricyanide all over it.

i do a lot of burning and dodging when making a print and then use bleach. there's not a straight print in the TULSA book. when i'm photographing i always try to shoot against the light (Figure 4). the film can't handle this and everything gets burned up, since i'm exposing for the shadows. in the darkroom i'll print for the shadow and then burn in everything else. i get as much light in the print as i can and then develop it sometimes as short as forty-five seconds. i get good grays this way and then use some bleach on the highlights to pick up the contrast. i get a better three dimensional quality in my prints and that makes them look sharper, without the help of in-focus developer.

in all the years i've been printing i've seen everybody do everything different. but if it works for you, it works. when i worked for walter sheffer i'd soup all the 2¼ rolls of film by hand in a big five gallon vat of homemade developer called hammer. a great developer for tri-x. i'd do twenty rolls at a time with no reels. i wore a coat with three pockets for the overexposed, normal, and underexposed film. after i'd stripped the backing paper off and had the naked film in my three pockets, i'd unroll a roll and slide it into the developer, where it would roll back up. first the under, then the normal, and then the over. after all twenty rolls were in the soup, i'd reach in up to my elbows for a roll, unroll it, and slide it into a second vat of hammer. when all the film was in the second vat, i'd repeat the process and go back into the first vat. i had to do this fast, and when the timer went off i'd scuffle to get the film in the vat of stop bath and then hypo. this worked great and i very seldom got a scratch. like i said, if it works for you, it works. there ain't no rules. here's the formula for hammer developer:

hammer plate company, st. louis, 1890 elon (soft developer) — ½ oz. sodium sulfite (preservative, used to preserve meat) — 4 oz. hydraquinone (black developer) — 1 oz. sodium carbonite (an alkali for blacks) — 3 oz. borax (you can use kodak or 20 mule team. this is for fine grain) — 3 oz. potassium bromide (slows developer to prevent fog) — ¾ oz.
mix in one gallon water

one part hammer to two and one-half parts water. for hammer replenisher, use same formula for one gallon of mix but leave out the potassium bromide. the reason is because of the silver bromide buildup in the developer. use the replenisher straight. don't dilute.

the thing about making good prints is experience. studying with a master is the best way to learn. i was lucky to work with walter sheffer, because he's a great printer and a master of light. when i manipulate a print in the darkroom i'm just compensating for the film's failure to handle the kind of light i like to use. i'm just printing it back to the way it looked when i took the picture. if the film can't handle it, i can in the darkroom. gene smith once said, "a straight print is a drugstore print." i like drugstores but i think he meant it's just too easy, lazy. don't be dictated to by a machine. maybe it's not pure but i'll do anything to a print to get it like i want it. burn in, hold back, bleach, even crop. i know photographers who are so into giving the appearance of never cropping that they leave the black line around the print. but when they have a photograph that needs cropping, they'll crop and then mask in a phony black line around the print so they won't blow their image of purity. there are no rules, so don't box yourself into a corner. i experiment still. i like to print and have fun in the darkroom.

here's a picture of joe cocker (Figure 5), where i printed his face on the towel. it was easy to do. i just cut a hole in a piece of black paper and after making the overall exposure, i changed negatives and burned in the second face. it reminds me of the face of christ on veronica's veil.

i think a great print of a great photograph is better to look at than a lousy print of the same photograph. it's still a great photograph either way, but the good print gives me much more to get into while seeing the image, space, light, feeling of the photograph, i see the craft of the print. i love the medium. i even like these guys — sometimes (Figure 6).

here is walter sheffer's formula for a dynamite developer to use with portriga rapid No. 4, 118, 111, and record rapid:

develop paper at 100 F. repeat: that's 100 F elon — 1 oz. sodium sulfite — 6 oz. hydraquinone — 1 oz. sodium carbonite — 6 oz. potassium bromide — 1 oz.
mix in one gallon water

you can see sheffer's a good poker player
(that's aces over sixes).

FILM	ASA RATING	DEVELOPER	SOLUTION & TIME	AGITATION
Tri-X	200 to 1200	Hammer ——— Acufine	10 minutes 68 F ——— 5½ minutes 68 F	10 seconds in every minute ——— Roll tank on its side

ENLARGER	LENS	LIGHT SOURCE	USUAL APERTURE	USUAL EXPOSURE
Focomat 1C	EL-Nikkor 50mm *f*/2.8	No. 213	*f*/8	Varies

PAPER	DEVELOPER	SOLUTION & TIME	STOP BATH	FIXER
Polycontrast F	Defender ——— Dektol	1:1 ——— 2 to 4 minutes	28% glacial acetic acid solution* ——— 15 seconds	Kodak F-5 ——— 2 baths ——— 5 minutes in each

WASH	TONING	DRYING	FLATTENING	PRESENTATION
5 minutes running water ——— 5 minutes Perma Wash ——— 15 minutes final wash	None	Air dry on fresh blotters**	Prints are drymounted	None

*To make 28% solution, dilute 3 parts full strength glacial acetic acid with 8 parts water (96cc of 28% glacial acetic acid solution : 2000cc water). Glacial acetic acid is harmful to skin and respiratory tract. Do not breathe fumes or allow to spatter skin.

**Blotters must be inspected and replaced frequently. Stains on blotters will transfer to prints.

Figure 3: GENE SMITH

Figure 4: DEAD, 1970

Figure 5: POP STAR

Figure 6.

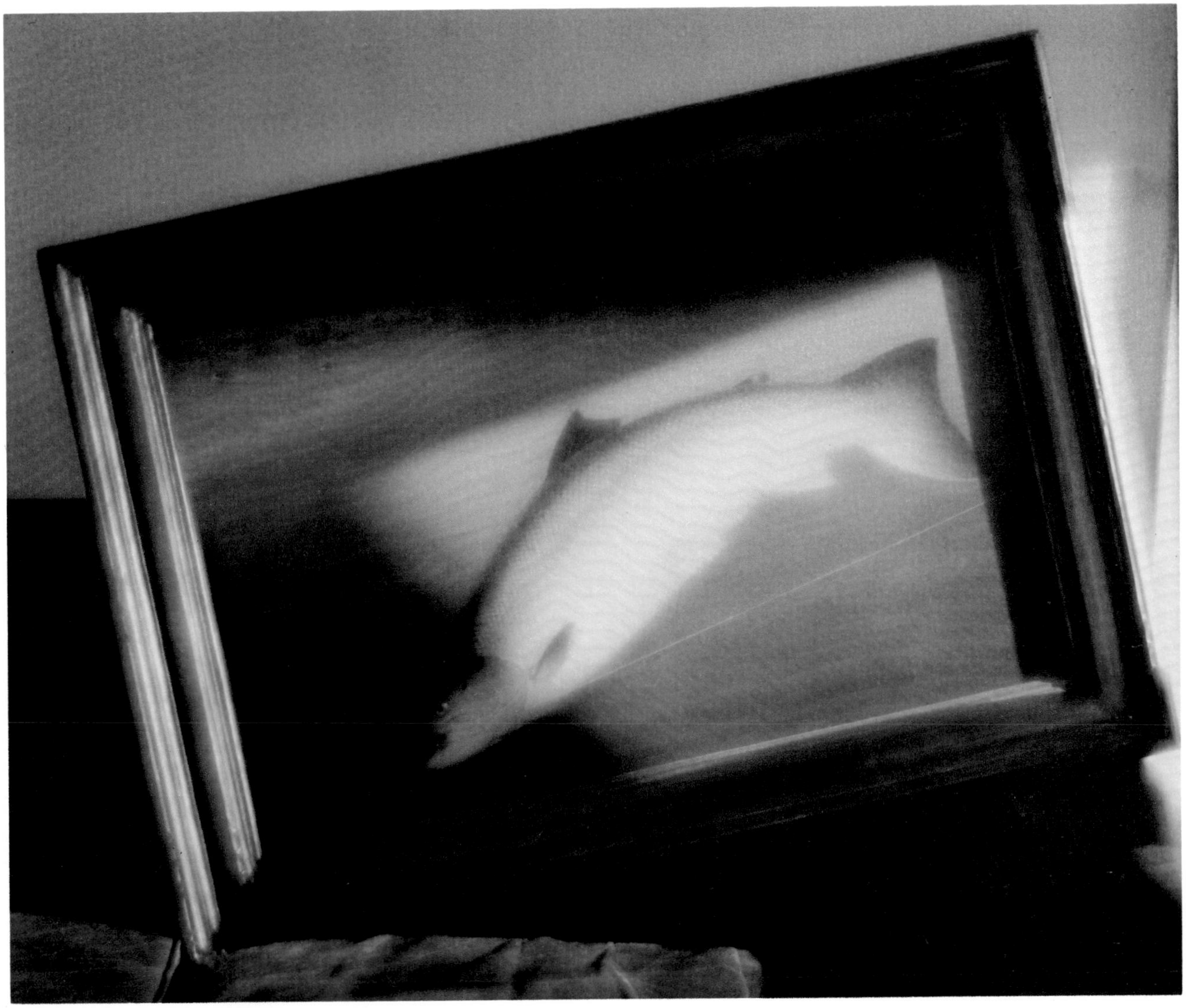

LINDA CONNOR

Linda Connor was born in New York City in 1944. She began photographing while in high school and got her first real camera, an Argus C-3, at the age of seventeen. In 1962, she enrolled in the Rhode Island School of Design where she joined the photography program and studied with Harry Callahan. In 1966 she went to graduate school, studying with Aaron Siskind at the Chicago Art Institute. Connor received her MS there and moved to San Francisco. Since 1969 she has been teaching at the San Francisco Art Institute and giving workshops. She received a National Endowment for the Arts grant in 1976.

Selected one-woman shows:

1969: Dayton Art Institute, Dayton, Ohio

1971: Focus Gallery, San Francisco
School of the Chicago Art Institute

1972: San Francisco Art Institute

1973: Light Gallery, New York

1974: Tyler School of Art, Philadelphia, Pennsylvania

1975: 218 Gallery, Memphis, Tennessee
Center Gallery, University of California, Berkeley Extension, San Francisco
Slightly Sloping Gallery, Visual Studies Workshop, Rochester, New York

1976: Spectrum Gallery, Tucson, Arizona
Susan Spiritus Gallery, Long Beach, California

Selected collections:

International Museum of Photography at George Eastman House, Rochester, New York
Art Institute of Chicago
Rhode Island School of Design, Providence
National Gallery of Canada, Ottawa
Musée Reàttu, Arles, France
Boston Museum of Fine Arts
Dallas Museum of Fine Arts, Dallas, Texas
Visual Studies Workshop, Rochester, New York
Museum of The University of New Mexico, Albuquerque
Fogg Art Museum, Cambridge, Massachusetts
Yale Art Museum, New Haven, Connecticut

Figure 1.

I decided to call myself a photographer about twelve years ago. My work and I have gone through many stages and changes since then. The work and process that I discuss here are my most recent. There is naturally some carryover from what preceded it (photographs of photographs, still lifes, setups, and all sorts of manipulations and combinations thereof). My shift into this new work happened unexpectedly a couple of years ago when I was given a camera which had belonged to a great-aunt. She had studied photography with Clarence White in 1905. The camera had been carefully packed away in an attic for years and, aside from a couple of leaks in the bellows, was in perfect shape — a cherrywood 8 x 10 Century with a shutterless, soft focus portrait lens. I only had to look through this lens once to know that I was hooked. It is an uncoated single element set in a long brass barrel. For exposures, I simply remove and replace the purple-lined lens cap (Figure 1). Ah, the silent click. Soon I was outfitted with cut film holders (the ones with the camera were for glass plates) and I discovered that this camera was unlike anything I could imagine. Looking through it and seeing the soft exploding colors on the ground glass was incredibly exciting.

As I began working, I realized that there were many limitations and eccentricities inherent in this "new" equipment. I found I had to change to a slower type of film. My hand was only so fast with the lens cap. I had to shoot on sunny days, when there would be lots of highlights. It was only with highlights that the uncoated lens produced those great halos and globs of light. Dull scenes came out so flat they looked like mud. I found I was working with an extremely narrow depth of field; it was a fairly "long" lens to begin with, having been designed for portraits. A set of brass waterhouse stops that came with the camera could increase depth of field, but as they cut down on the soft focus effect, I decided not to use them. After all, if I was going to work soft, it might as well be really soft, not just a little mushy. The amazing thing about the lens is that whatever is in focus is sharp and detailed, but at the same time a soft glow radiates from it.

The lack of deep focus had become one of the most interesting problems: what should be in or out of focus? Do I focus before, on, or behind an object? This alters the haloing and the way it looks. If a small object or line is near the lens and is totally out of focus, you can see right through it. It dissolves and becomes partially transparent.

Weight, bulk, and slowness became a consideration. When the bellows of the camera is cranked out all the way, it measures over three feet long! Then with the tripod and backpack for film holders—we are talking about a hell of a lot of equipment. I'm no Amazon, so I usually drive to an area, set up, and work for a while. Backyards and small

Figure 2.

Figure 3.

parks are about the right size. It is slow work. If you are interested in capturing the flux of life and action, this is not the equipment for you. Luckily, I am content to leave that aspect of photography to others.

One of the first types of pictures I attempted was the flat still life I had been working with earlier. But by the time the bellows were extended three feet, and I was up on a chair, just to be able to see into the ground glass, with the camera pointed down at the objects I was shooting, well, we all had a tendency to tip over. It was so harrowing that I succumbed to landscapes, which were straight ahead and generally exciting and unexplored territory for me.

Probably the most dramatic change in my work (besides how these pictures looked) was the way I went about making them. Before, I partially thought out the image or the basic idea behind it. Then I would set it up. I always had some idea before I started, even if I changed it radically in process. But now I was using equipment that did more than just frame and render the reality before it. This camera demanded to see and do things in its own manner. It was very difficult to know what was going to work out well before looking through the camera. The most unexpected things might be right. I was no longer daydreaming ideas and images; I was out trudging around with this clumsy camera, hunting them. It was a different way for me to work, and a good change.

I tray develop, usually six sheets of film at a time. I use two trays side by side, passing the sheets back and forth; I get fewer scratches with this system. If I really worried about scratches, I would develop one sheet at a time, but I'm too impatient. I develop with Dektol — it's quick, contrasty, and always around. My development time is about five minutes, using a solution of 150 cc Dektol to 1000 cc water. I Sometimes vary this dilution after seeing the first batch of film by splashing in some more Dektol when the negatives look thin. I hate to measure and be accurate, so they often come out a little different. I fix, hypo clear, and wash like a good girl.

Most of my negatives are so dense that you need a strong light behind them to see what's there (Figure 2). The density occurs from working without a shutter, wide open on sunny days. I also have to develop fully for a contrasty image. The paper I use has a wide range of tones, even less contrast than a No. 1 paper, so this added contrast is needed.

I contact print using old-fashioned print frames with hinged backs so I can see how it's coming along (Figure 3). I have five of these frames and usually print out on my back porch, but when the weather looks tricky I'll use window light. My exposures vary considerably depending on the time of year (it takes longer in the winter), the time of day, general weather conditions — clouds, shadows, etc. It can take less than ten minutes to expose a thin negative and up to three days for an extremely dense one. You just keep checking the progress, taking a quick peek by opening one half of the back of the frame (Figure 4).

I use Print-out paper (P.O.P. or, as Kodak calls it, "Studio Proof"). Sunlight turns it dark, lovely shades of red, purple, and green. It does everything by itself — no development, just light. After the print is exposed, if left in the light, it will continue to get darker, but it can be fixed and made permanent. The paper is designed for studio photographers to send out as proofs. These proofs self-destruct so the customers have to buy real prints. If you want more than a transient proof, you must fix it. I also tone the image, because the fixing process gives the print an awful orange color. These wet processes tend to bleach back and lighten, so the print must be considerably overexposed to begin with. It takes a little practice to be able to judge when a print is done just right.

During exposure, the paper (which you can handle safely in shade or room light) turns from white to pink, shades of maroon, a reddish brown, and finally, if it's had lots of sun, an olive green. I normally print until the shadow areas of the picture are olive green. The rest of the image is usually dark maroon with a little pink in the highlights. After exposure, I put the prints in a box for safekeeping until I can get around to toning them. As long as they stay pretty much out of the light, they will be fine almost indefinitely. It's a lovely process — no more smelly darkroom. In fact, once the film is developed, everything else is done in the light.

I tone in the bathroom because the water runs there, but any place with water and room for some trays will do. Room light is fine and almost necessary since the process is so long and boring, you might as well enjoy a good book. I usually tone two prints at a time in separate trays. If I do more than one print in a tray, I tend to get uneven toning.

First, prepare a tray of plain hypo (sodium thiosulfite). I usually add about a cup of hypo crystals to a quart of hot water; the water cools as the crystals dissolve, leaving you with a solution at about the correct temperature. I don't bother using a thermometer. I just make sure that nothing is too hot. You need to use plain hypo rather than regular fixer, because the latter is too strong and bleaches the image.

The toner is gold chloride, and it is expensive. The price went up about 300 percent in 1974. I just thought I'd warn you. Anyway, you take a fifteen grain vial of gold chloride and with the little file the chemist will give you, you carefully file it open. Then, put the gold chloride, vial and all (so as not to waste any crystals that might be sticking to the glass), into a beaker of 500 cc of water (use bottled water if yours is rusty). The crystals will dissolve easily. Now filter it into a bottle marked "A-gold." You'll also need a second chemical,

Figure 4.

ammonium thiocyanate; mix up 10 grams with 500 cc of water. I don't have a scale, but I've found that if you fill a plastic Kodak 35mm film cassette can with the chemical, you come out about right. Put this in a second bottle labeled "B-A.T." These two bottles contain your stock solutions. Now mix up 50 cc of A, 50 cc of B, and add 500 cc of water. Pour this into one or two trays and you are ready to go.

First the prints must be washed in cold water for a few minutes until the milky stuff stops coming off the print. (I think this is excess silver.) Pre-wash for three to five minutes. Drain and place the print in the toning solution (yes, you tone first, then fix), agitating the whole time. I find that rocking the tray is the best way to do this, since tongs or fingers often crease or scratch the print surface. The emulsion of this paper is very soft when wet, and it comes only in single weight, so you must be particularly careful when handling it. Even fingerprints will affect the toning. (It is extremely prissy paper.) Once in the toner, the print will quickly change from maroon to an orange and the image will get much lighter. As the toning progresses, the orange will start turning gray-brown, the color of the toned print. You can see it happen. If the gold is fresh, it takes five to ten minutes a print, but as the solution gets used up, it takes considerably longer. As the gold leaves the solution, the tone of the prints will shift. They will become warmer and more orange. The first few prints in a new solution of gold are usually a purple-gray, the next few are browner, and the last couple quite orange.

Now I put the prints into hypo for about six minutes, where they will again get a little lighter. Next I put them in a water bath and hold them there until I have a big enough batch to hypo clear and wash. I use a washer that holds the prints separately, but a tray siphon would also work. (Just be careful the prints don't get creased.) When they are through washing in thirty to forty minutes, I drain them and place them in pairs, back to back. Then I hang them by the corners with plastic clothespins. They air dry in a few hours, and will always curl, but, if pressed with a couple of heavy books, they flatten out in a couple of days. (Do not dry these prints in a heat dryer — the image will transfer to the apron.) Finally, I dry mount the prints on thin boards slightly larger than the prints, because I find they are just too thin without some backing. I then spot them and if I like the image enough, I overmatte it. The casualty rate on these prints from start to finish is pretty high. Getting the exposure right, the toning even, the color you like, no creases, these are some of the problems you face. Well, you lose a lot of prints. It is also close to impossible to get two prints to come out looking the same. I just don't worry about it. Each print is a little bit different and if I like it, fantastic. Oh, remember that green? Well, sometimes when the green is very intense on the print and the toner is partially depleted, the toner will plate up on those areas, giving it a kind of uneven surface, almost a solarized look. This can be really beautiful, but it is difficult to control or describe.

Why do I go to all this trouble and expense to gold tone on Print-out Paper when I could contact print on another kind of paper? It would be easier to use another paper, but the prints would look very different. The P.O.P. renders the image with a delicacy that is hard to match (Figure 5). Maybe I'm a little tired of plain old black and white prints, but I really like the brown tones the gold produces. These prints have a warm receptive quality that I've never found in regular silver bromide prints. Each print is unique in tone and intensity. I would like the print to be a new object, not just a neutral reflection, reference, or record of reality. I want people to look at the print and to be satisfied with it.

As this is not the equipment one would use to record information-packed images anyway, I found that the content or subject of these pictures became less and less important (Figure 6). If it looked good enough, that's all that mattered to me. Interesting things started to happen in relation to these low content images. I became aware that if the content was reduced, the look and structure of the picture had to be stronger. In a way, the content of these images became the structure and the appearance of the print.

The idea that photographs always give visual information and reflect reality directly is a hard one to shake. Often my images, which do not hold much content and which alter visual information because of lens aberration, seem to hold a hidden mystery (Figure 7). They have the quality of an old map of some unknown location, or a nameless family album.

The first landscapes with this camera were just too beautiful. I had gone overboard. My romantic nature and my notion of what soft focus photo-successionist work looks like, combined with this soft lens, made the pictures drip with honey. I realized I wanted something more interesting, something that might look beautiful, but that also had an edge to it, some teeth. The lens could supply the beauty. I had to supply the edge. I could take a battered trash can with a couple of poles leaning on it and make it work as an image. What I needed to find was a balance and, in my best pictures, I feel it's there (Figure 8).

This way of making pictures seems right for me for the time being. There is still much to discover about my particular camera and the visual applications it may hold in store. When I feel I understand my pictures and this equipment, I will move on to something different; but for now I'm working hard and I'm content.

FILM	ASA RATING	DEVELOPER	SOLUTION & TIME	AGITATION
Kodak Ektapan: 8x10	None	Dektol ——— 70 F	Dektol 150cc: water — 1000cc ——— 5 minutes or until done	Continuous ——— 2 flat bottom 8x10 trays, shifting sheet film back and forth

ENLARGER	LENS	LIGHT SOURCE	USUAL APERTURE	USUAL EXPOSURE
None	None	Sun	None	10 minutes to 3 days, depending on weather conditions and negative density

PAPER	DEVELOPER	SOLUTION & TIME	STOP BATH	FIXER
Kodak Studio Proof (P.O.P.) ——— F surface	Sun	None	None	Sodium thiosulfite ——— 1 cup crystals: hot water — 1 quart ——— 6 minutes

WASH	TONING	DRYING	FLATTENING	PRESENTATION
5 minutes prewash ——— 2 to 5 minutes hypo eliminator ——— 30 minutes final tray wash	Gold Chloride*	Air dry	Face to face under weights	Drymount on thin museum board ——— Overmatte with museum board ——— Under glass

*To tone, wash print in tray of cold, running water for 5 minutes. Tone one print at a time in tray of solution. Tone until even (about 10 minutes). Agitate continually. Do not touch print at this stage. Drain, place toned print in tray of plain hypo (without hardener) and fix for 6 minutes. Wash, hypo clear, final wash and air dry.

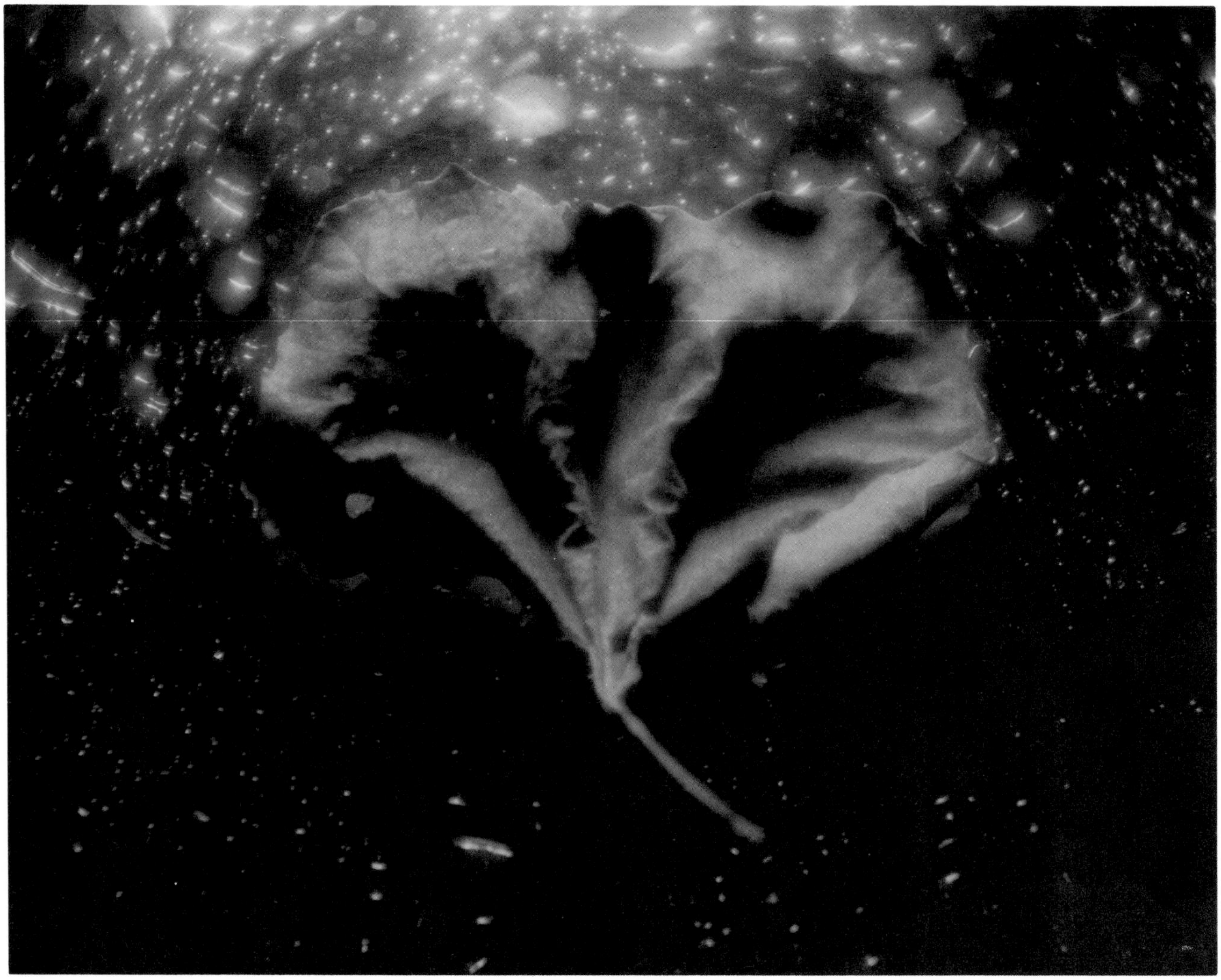

Figure 5.

Figure 6.

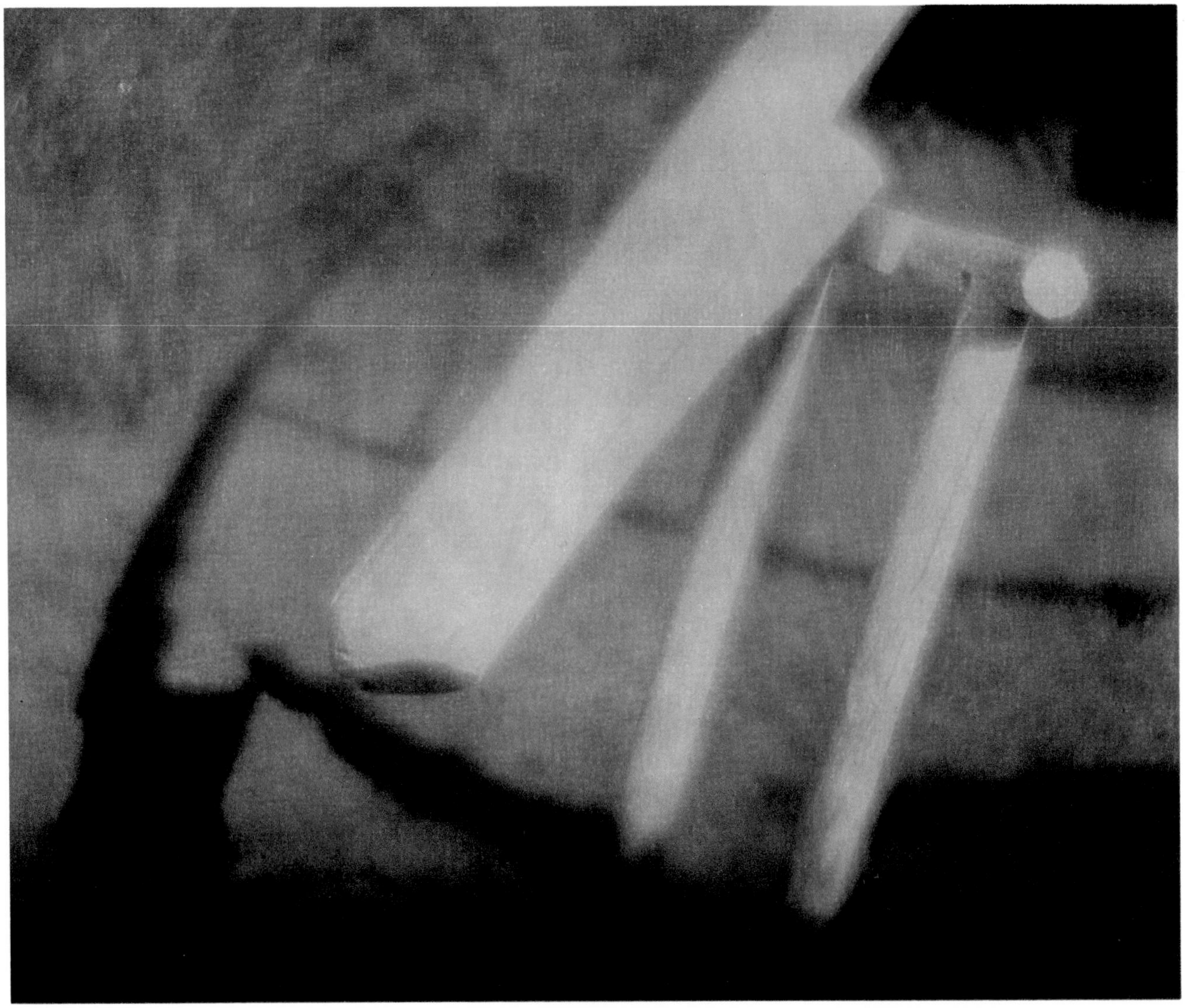

Figure 7.

Figure 8.

RALPH GIBSON

Ralph Gibson was born in Los Angeles in 1939. He grew up in Hollywood and joined the Navy in 1956. Discharged from the Navy in 1960, he studied at the San Francisco Art Institute. He became assistant to Dorothea Lange in 1962. In 1966, his book, THE STRIP (Roger Kennedy, Los Angeles) was published and he moved to New York to work with Robert Frank. In 1969 he founded Lustrum Press and published his own THE SOMNAMBULIST as well as LOUD SONG by Danny Seymour, TULSA by Larry Clark and PORTUGAL by Neal Slavin.

In 1972 DEJA-VU, Gibson's second self-published sequence, appeared. In 1973 and again in 1976, he won a National Endowment for the Arts grant. Lustrum Press published his third book, DAYS AT SEA, in 1975.

Selected one-man shows:

1970: San Francisco Art Institute

1972: Pasadena Museum of Art, Pasadena, California

1973: American Cultural Center, Paris
International Museum of Photography at George Eastman House, Rochester, New York

1974: Palais des Beaux Arts, Brussels

1975: Hoesch Museum, Duren, Germany
Galerie Agathe Gaillard, Paris
Madison Art Center, Madison, Wisconsin
Broxton Gallery, Los Angeles

1976: Leo Castelli Gallery-Castelli Graphics, New York
Museum of Modern Art, Stockholm, Sweden
Baltimore Museum of Art

Selected collections:
Bibliothèque Nationale, Paris
Museum of Modern Art, New York
Fort Worth Museum of Art, Fort Worth, Texas
The Museum of Fine Arts, Houston, Texas
International Museum of Photography at George Eastman House, Rochester, New York
Stedelijk Museum, Amsterdam, The Netherlands
Fogg Art Museum, Cambridge, Massachusetts
Seattle Art Museum, Seattle, Washington

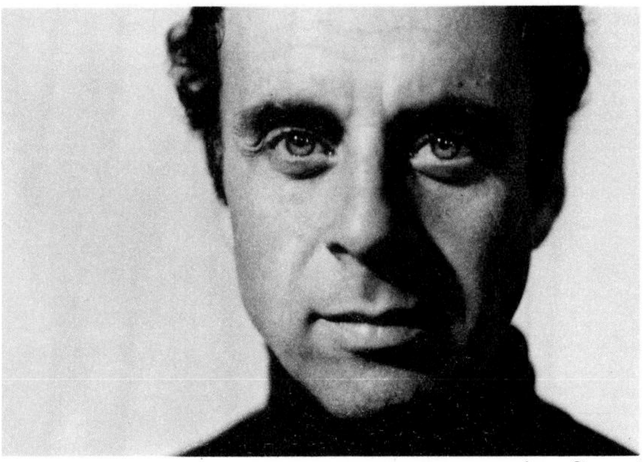

Amos Shepard

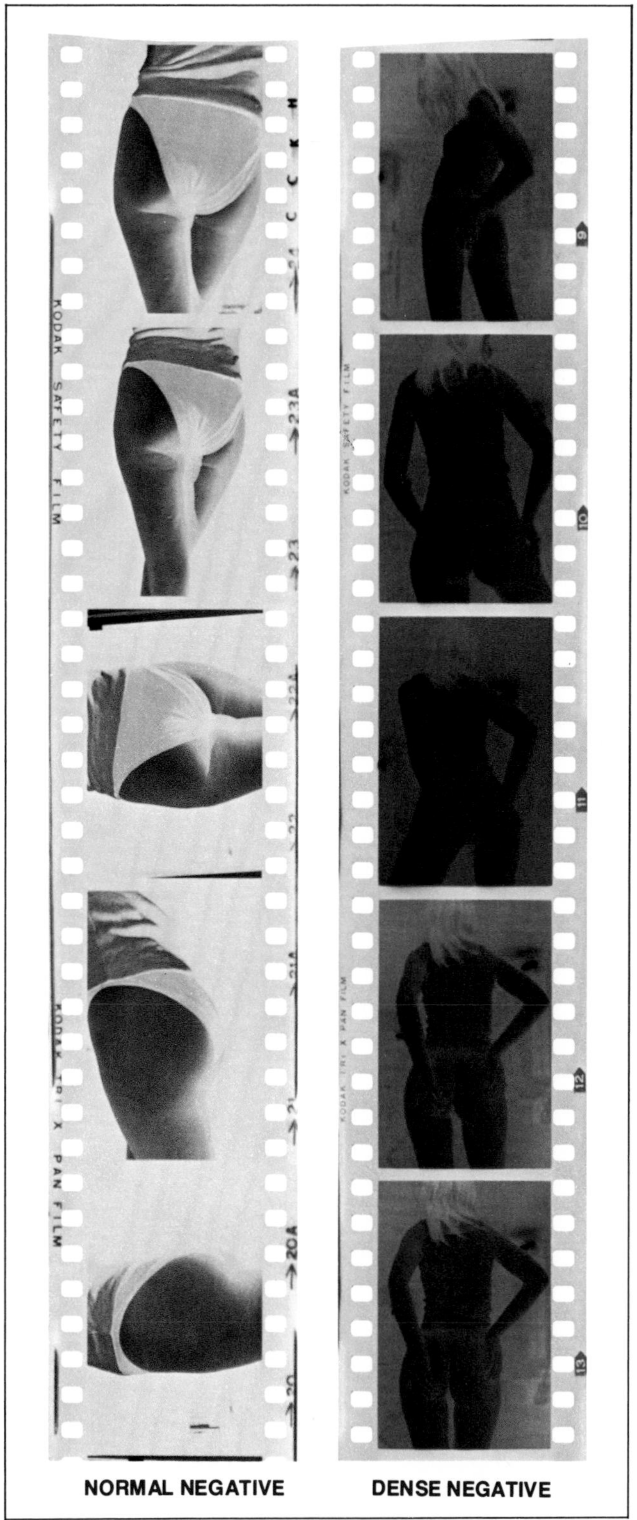

Figure 1.

Rather than take a photograph to document an event, I try to make a statement that happens to be, among other things, a photograph. The exposure of the negative and its printing are inherently related to the statement.

For many years I made what is called a normal negative, struggled with the materials and came up with an acceptable print. However, when THE SOMNAMBULIST was on the press, I discovered that by adding more ink I could achieve certain contrast relationships in reproduction that I couldn't get with my normal negatives. I had been searching for this look for ten years. When the lithographer started adding ink to the plates I realized that it was possible to get those big solid blacks. Having learned from the lithographic process I now go directly to contrasty subject matter and expose for the narrow contrast ratio I desire. I overexpose and overdevelop and, in the process, pick up grain and contrast. This yields a dense negative (Figure 1), but through the years I have found that I prefer them this way. A dense negative offers a range of possibilities that, when explored, yields greater content.

I'm interested in acutance as well as strong contrast and therefore use a high contrast paper. This also accentuates the grain, a textural concern which is related to spatial effect. For example, I could take a shot with a 21mm lens and produce gross spatial distortion. But I'm not interested in having a kind of "lensy" space. I don't want the lens to do it, I want to do it with my eye. I have used the 50mm lens exclusively for several years and find that it holds the perspectives I want. I can alter the light through developing and printing to produce the psychological effect I require. I project my internal concerns onto external reality. Technical considerations relate to content.

An important aspect of the nature of photography is its capacity to reduce a large three-dimensional universe to a much smaller two-dimensional plane. I've always been concerned with how to suggest the third dimension in my two-dimensional art. At one time I used wide lenses for their distorted spatial effects. Now I prefer the 50mm lens, which is virtually free of distortion in its ability to render three-dimensional objects in space.

For the past seven or eight years I've been trying to tighten the frame, to fill it more and more. At a certain point I realized that only a small fragment of the entire scene was stimulating my eye—a collar, or the buttons on a shirt—so I moved in on these details. Photographing close up eliminates the possibility of both happy and unhappy accidents either enhancing or ruining the image. I feel a great need to be fully aware of and responsible for everything in the frame.

I used to stand around waiting for a picture to happen. Then about fifteen years ago, Dorothea Lange told me that you can never take photographs that way. Even though it will sometimes happen, the odds are stacked against you. You have to incorporate your life into the picture. Now I'm always working from a set of concerns. It could be problems involving scale, volume, proportions, or surface. I perceive something and experience the urge to photograph it. I try to decide whether I've done the picture before. (I don't want to imitate myself.) If it's a step forward within these concerns, I take the photograph.

Learning to use the camera is much like learning to play a musical instrument, except that a camera is simpler. Any photographer should be able to change exposures without looking at the camera. There are just a couple of knobs and dials. It's easy to memorize the number of clicks in the click-stop diaphragm. Start at *f*/2 and train your fingers moving down to *f*/16 or *f*/22. Even if you are a stop or two off in either direction, the negative will be printable. For a long time, I've practiced turning the lens-focusing barrel so that I can come close to where I want the lens to be focused and have only a minor adjustment to make as the camera reaches my eye. I've also learned to read light by guessing exposures and then taking a meter reading. All the problems of pulling out the exposure meter, looking at the camera, and turning knobs can be eliminated.

To develop Tri-X, I use 10 cc of Rodinal for every roll. If I am developing two rolls of film in a two-reel tank, I fill the tank with water at 68 degrees to within a quarter of an inch of the brim. Then I pour in 20 cc of developer and stir. This is generally considered too harsh a solution, but it gives me the quality I desire. An eleven minute development time with agitation every minute and a half for ten seconds yields a contrasty negative having the appearance of blocked highlights. Thinner negatives, finer grain, longer development . . . I've tried all these approaches, but the only negative that I consider interesting in terms of its potential is the overexposed, overdeveloped one.

Because I almost always shoot in bright sun on Tri-X with the camera set for *f*/16, there's a uniformity to my negatives. I start printing on either Brovira No. 4 or No. 5 paper with a fifteen second exposure and the El-Nikkor enlarger lens at *f*/5.6. When I print, I think of the will of the negative and how I should respond to it. While the image is fixed, the light can be manipulated. Even when I'm making the first exposure on the first sheet of paper, I try to imagine the light rays from the enlarger penetrating the emulsion of the paper. When I develop, I imagine the developer softening and penetrating the emulsion of the film or paper. That's also the way I think when I expose film in the camera. Looking through the range finder, I'll imagine millions of rays of light going through the lens and burning into the film. This attitude brings me into closer contact with the materials. I like to think of the energy, the speed, and the meaning of the entire process. I could never give anybody else my negatives to print, because they wouldn't make the same decisions. Printing is not only a question of skill, it's a question of attitude.

The BLOND MAN WITH A BEARD (Figure 3) was standing behind a glass door about an inch thick. The quality of light is transformed as it moves through the glass because the glass acts as a condenser, focusing the light rays. Light is coming over my shoulder through the glass, playing on the surface of the man's face, bouncing back through the glass of the door into the camera lens and onto the film, then back through the glass of the enlarger lens onto the paper. When I took the photograph, I exposed for the highlights and let the shadows go black, as always. Shadow detail is of great concern to some photographers. It's something I don't like in my work. I prefer to have the shadows go completely black to produce strong shapes.

What accounts for the quality of the man's expression is the way he is placed within the frame. I made the negative on Tri-X using a Leica M-3 with a dual-range 50mm Summicron lens. This dual-range Summicron enables me to focus in closer, which I like because I am physically closer to the subject and I believe this proximity can be felt by the viewer. Many single-lens reflex cameras will focus even closer than the dual-range Summicron, but I prefer to work with the Leica. I have enjoyed relating to it for many years. I like the way the image looks through the optical glass of the viewfinder, and I'm familiar with the translation. The picture comes out the way I saw it, which is the big thing in photography, to get what you see. However, I think at the moment the camera shutter clicks there is a tremendous unknown.

Often while working in the darkroom I'll make a print and put it up on a sheet of glass to study. I try to gauge how I respond to the image, looking at it perhaps through a reducing glass (Figure 2), or maybe putting my face very close to the surface of the print to see what the elements within the picture do, and what would improve the print. The paper I used here is No. 5 Brovira III. I like having a glossy surface which I dry matte. This enables me to get a colder and deeper black.

The DOORMAN (Figure 4) was fairly complicated to print. The negative was my usual Tri-X, bright sun combination of *f*/16 at 1/250. I wanted to reinforce the blacks overall, so I burned in the triangle in the upper left hand corner for an additional fifteen seconds. I felt there was too much texture in the coat and decided to darken this area with another thirty second exposure. The bricks seemed too hot, so I took them down for fifteen seconds overall, making sure that the hair didn't receive light in the process. These decisions came slowly over a long period of printing. I recall making about twenty prints before I found the balance and tonality I was trying to achieve.

The robe in the window is called SELF-PORTRAIT (Figure 5) because it seems to resemble something it perhaps isn't. This situation is entirely different from the BLOND MAN WITH THE BEARD, because it is night time and the light source is artificial. The negative is more difficult to print. I wanted to keep the white piping of the robe very white and the rest of it deep black. The robe had to be burned in around the sash, and the background also required attention in order to produce an even tonality and balance. The robe didn't look as much like a figure when I originally saw it, and it didn't have the same presence. This is why printing is such an interesting phenomenon. It permits the photographer to discover the potential of the negative. For example, the fact that the screen was too light was something the print told me.

In the photograph of THE TORSO (Figure 6), several concerns came together simultaneously. As I made the print, I was trying to suggest some kind of pulse in the figure, her heartbeat, and I noticed that by having a highlight on the left and a shadow on the right there would be a certain stroboscopic effect that carries the eye back and forth. It is possible to see motion in this photograph. Then, as I looked at the 11 x 14 print, I realized that my eye was the same distance from the print as my camera had been from the original subject, and that the image was within half an inch of the size of the original subject. Making a photograph the size of the object photographed is not terribly unique. However, about 99 percent of all photographs taken, do in fact, reduce the size of the original. Here I discovered that in order to get that feeling of heat and the texture of the skin and the pulse of the organs, the scale ratio had to be one to one.

I couldn't quite get the skin tones that I wanted. If I underexposed the paper, I couldn't get certain blacks and shadows. If I overexposed it, I immediately got the wrong kind of contrast, the wrong kind of blacks. I went back to my "normal" exposure, the fifteen second exposure I always start with when I'm examining a negative. The phone rang when I put the print into the developer. I had previously discovered that I could turn a print face down in the developer and briefly leave the darkroom. So I did this, making sure that the print sank to the bottom of the tray, and went and spoke on the phone for about seven minutes. When I came back into the darkroom, I cleared the print quickly and turned on the lights. To my surprise, I had reached the tone I had been searching for, one I couldn't get through normal exposure and development procedures. This technique also helped to emphasize the peculiar highlight called bromide drag on the right side of the hip and back. I've always liked

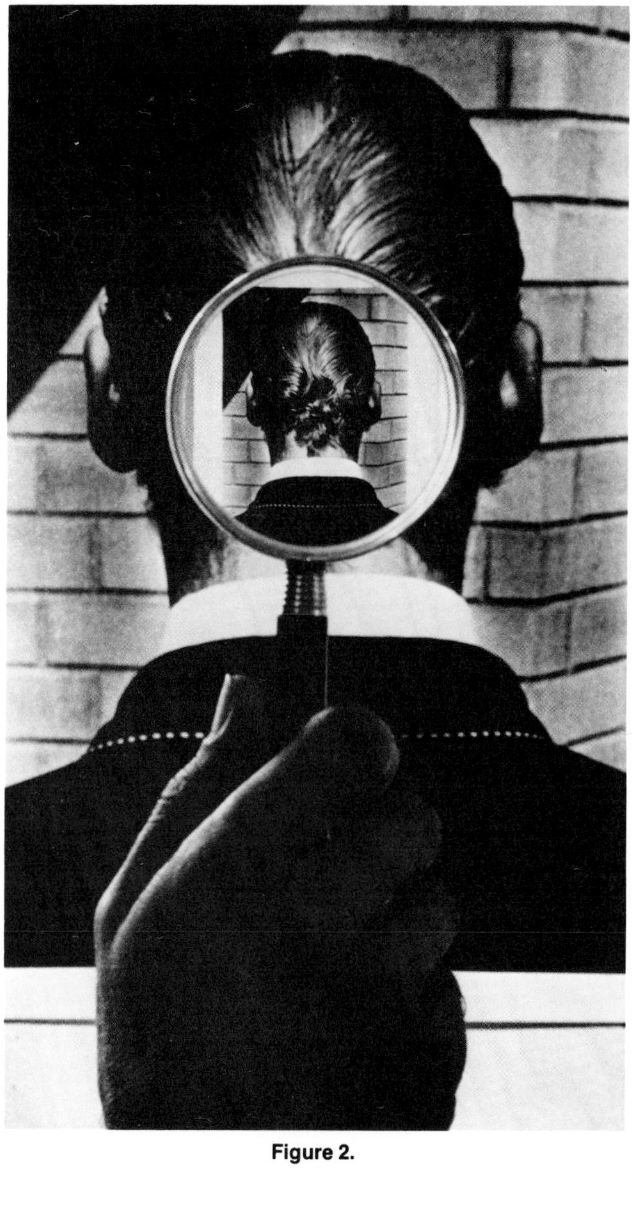

Figure 2.

the effect of bromide drag, and one of the ways I seem to retain it best is through minimal print agitation.

I have subsequently examined this technique of non-agitation and have discovered that if I agitate only for the first one-half minute, so that plenty of developer soaks into the paper and the emulsion is completely soft, I can get something equivalent to a middle grade of paper. I printed this on a No. 5 Brovira III. On a No. 4, it wouldn't have quite the snap, and if I printed it on a No. 5, with normal agitation, it would be too contrasty. Skin tones need a certain luminosity, which this procedure gives.

I like to think of my photographs as being their own source of light. I want them to radiate light, not necessarily reflect it. An interesting print can be viewed under almost any kind of lighting. This idea has led me to the use of strong contrast, because I think that big black areas and big white areas are more interesting in terms of what they do with light. As I look at the picture of THE TORSO, I feel that there's a translucent quality to the dark areas, and underneath the dark areas, some kind of energy is coming from the figure.

I slightly darkened the upper-left-hand corner of the print to balance it better with the right-hand corner. If I'm looking at a print, and there's something wrong but I don't know what it is, I'll examine the corners. If a corner is too light in value, it will drain energy away. My eye tends to go to the brightest part of the print, so I often burn in or darken the corners.

I make my prints 11 x 14 or 16 x 20 for exhibition purposes. However, when reproduced in a book, they are much smaller. Looking at a book of photographs is a different experience from looking at an exhibit. Almost everyone holds a book at about the same distance from their eyes, give or take six inches. Nobody pins a book up on the wall, walks away, and looks at it from across the room. A book provides a private experience. When you look at photographs reproduced in a book, you do it in a more tranquil moment, often at home, with little external distraction. You can adjust your viewing distance to exactly that point where reality pops into some kind of recognizable form for you. Certain psychological effects can be best experienced in this type of controlled viewing situation.

My primary concern in the photograph of THE PRIEST (Figure 7) was to formalize the composition as rigidly as possible. This required a decision as to how much black coat would be allowed to show and how it would balance with the almost identical negative shapes in the sky. The priest was posed in bright sun so that the geometric division of his collar would be intense. I recall wanting to keep the triangle a dense white . . . luminous and vibrating in front of the picture plane. Of course the overexposure and overdevelopment of the film produced this effect. I didn't want his coat to go completely black, but almost. I discovered this happened if I let the print develop out for a full three minutes. I wanted to make a statement, both religious and photographic, in a tight structural way.

The photograph of the CORNER OF A BUILDING (Figure 8) was made in Arles, in the south of France. It appeals to me for two reasons, one being the spatial statement it makes. There's a strong relationship between the negative space of the black on the left side of the frame and the architectural detail on the right. Many times I find myself looking at the black side more than the light side. The second reason is that there's no manipulation in the enlarging process. I simply put the negative in the enlarger, gave it the fifteen second exposure, developed the print, and came up with the best print for this negative. In eighteen years this had never happened. I am beginning to realize that making a tremendous effort in the darkroom both helps to perfect one's vision and to extract the maximum content from a given negative. If I work in the darkroom in the morning for two or three hours, and then go out and photograph, my eye is quicker and my awareness higher. The great amount of time I spend in the darkroom influences my vision at the moment I decide to take the photograph.

There has to be a reason why darkroom work is so important. It is easier to go around making photographs than it is to print and understand them. Quite often because of the speed of the shutter, the speed of the film, etc., I will have momentary peaks of awareness. Sometimes it is difficult to raise my perceptions to where they were in that fraction of a second. Darkroom work forces me to do so. In this way, I learn many things about how I see.

It's true that some photographers can successfully send their work to a commercial printer who understands what they're trying to say. But I've learned a great deal about how I perceive things from my time in the darkroom. I've also noticed that when I don't feel like printing I just set up the trays and the urge will come.

Photographers who do their own darkroom work come to understand certain things about the nature of the medium. (A negative may have visual flaws, and it is in the darkroom that we face them.) As my technical abilities increase, I hope that one day I will learn to perceive something in its totality at the moment I photograph. This is my ultimate goal. I'm certain that my approach can only be considered valid for my own needs. Having discussed the creative process with many photographers through the years has clearly shown me that no two workers approach the medium from the same direction. Different goals and different personalities require unique and personal methods of work. And everything is always changing.

FILM	ASA RATING	DEVELOPER	SOLUTION & TIME	AGITATION
Tri-X	100 to 400	Rodinal 68 F	1:25 11 minutes	10 seconds in every 1½ minutes Roll tank on its side

ENLARGER	LENS	LIGHT SOURCE	USUAL APERTURE	USUAL EXPOSURE
Focomat 1C	EL-Nikkor 50mm *f*/2.8	No. 212	*f*/5.6	15 seconds

PAPER	DEVELOPER	SOLUTION & TIME	STOP BATH	FIXER
Brovira III Nos. 4 and 5	Dektol	1:1 2½ to 3 minutes	28% glacial acetic acid solution 15 seconds	Kodak F-5 2 baths 5 minutes in each

WASH	TONING	DRYING	FLATTENING	PRESENTATION
5 minutes running water 5 minutes Perma Wash 15 minutes final wash	None	Air dry on fresh blotters	Sandwiched between fresh blotters, under weights	Drymount Under glass No frame

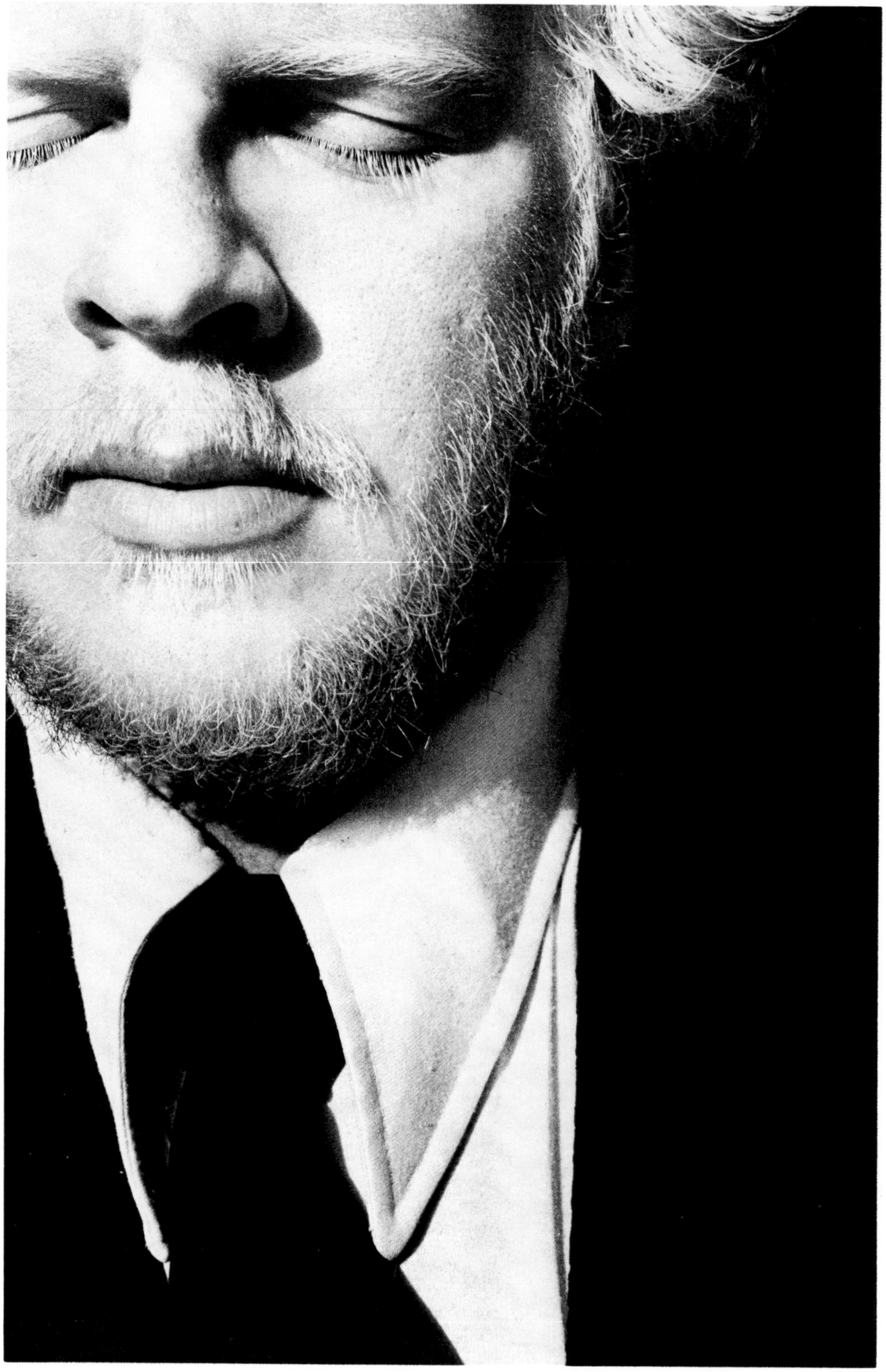

Figure 3: BLOND MAN WITH BEARD

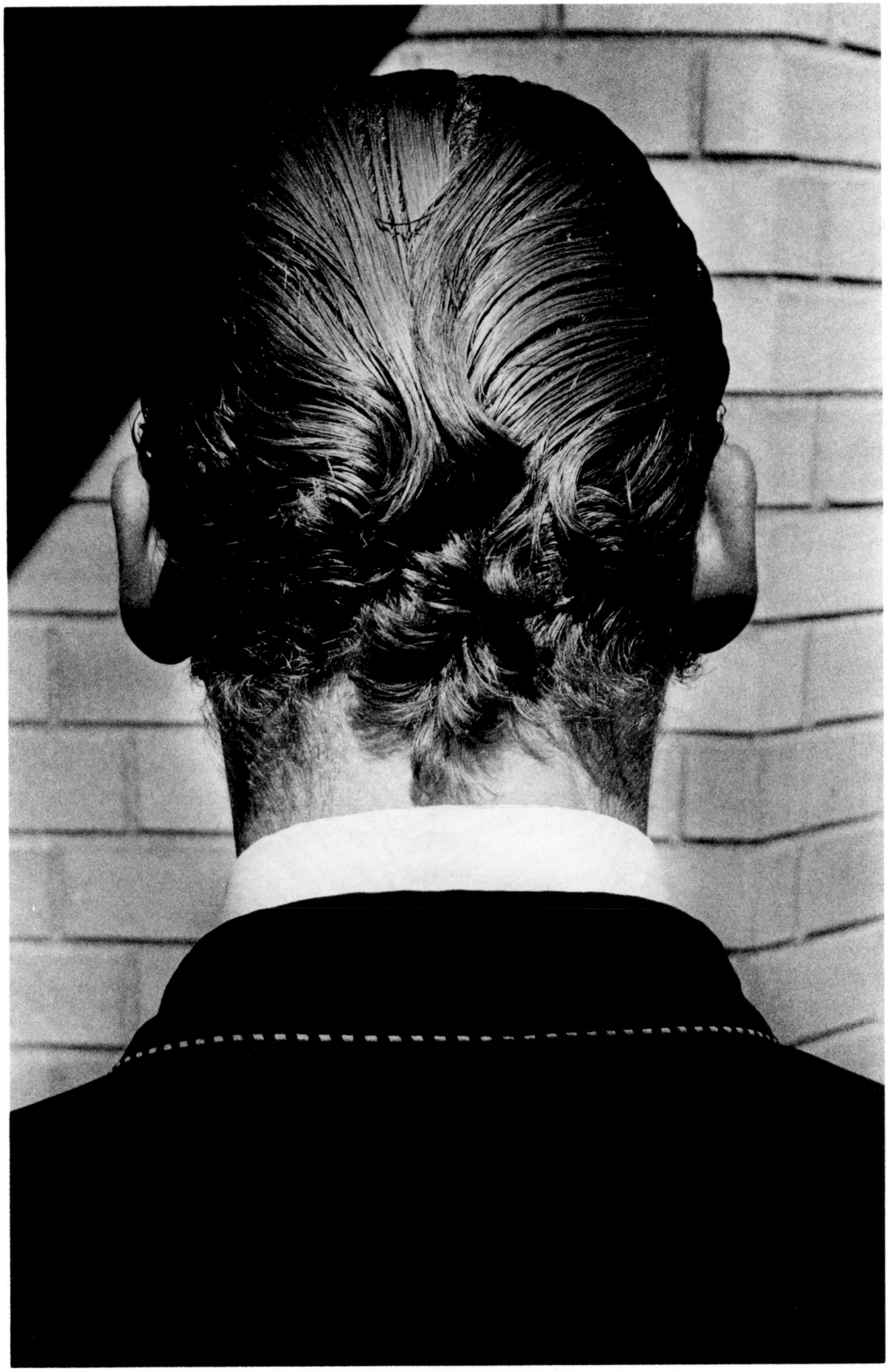

Figure 4: THE DOORMAN

Figure 5: SELF PORTRAIT

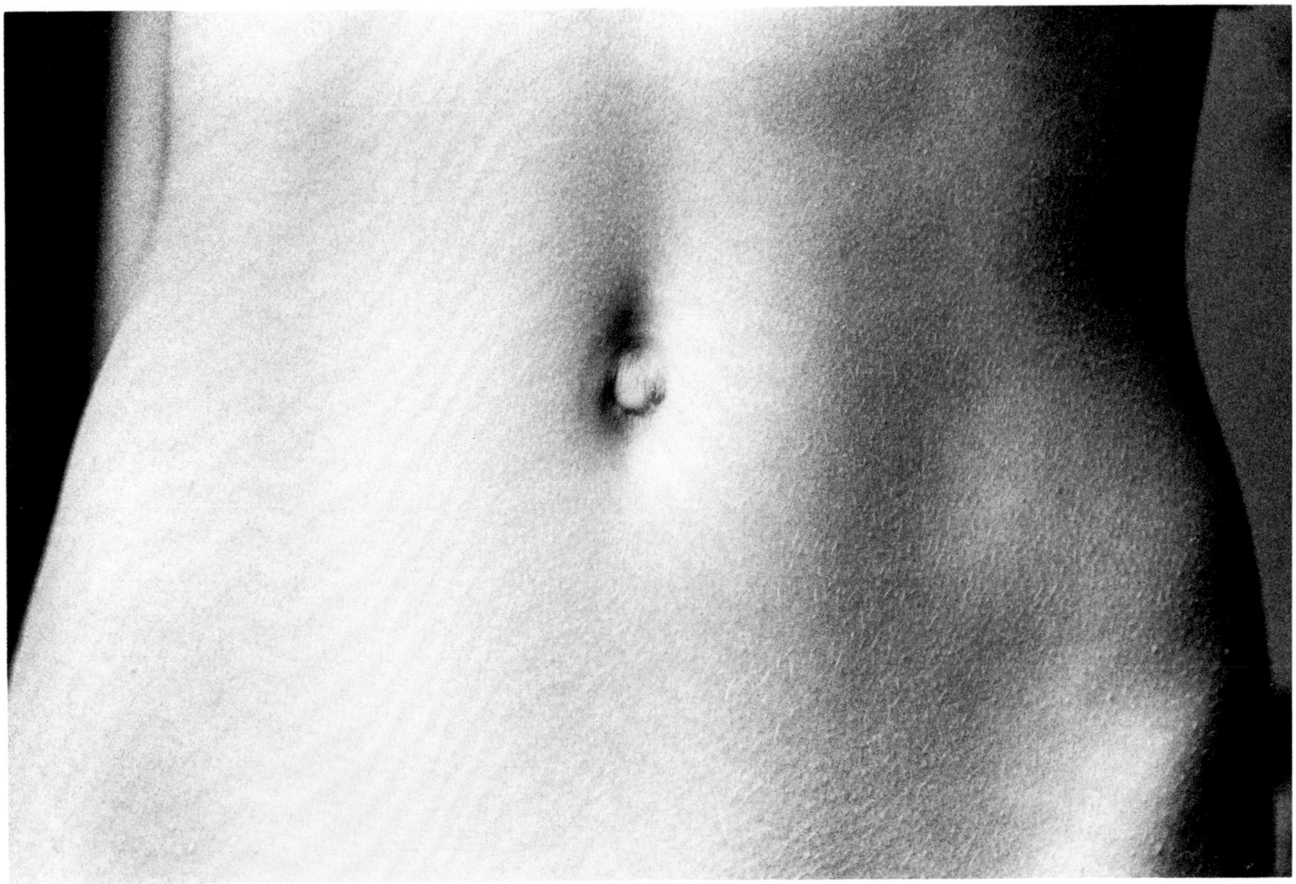

Figure 6: THE TORSO

Figure 7: THE PRIEST

Figure 8: CORNER OF BUILDING

BETTY HAHN

Betty Hahn was born in Chicago in 1940. On graduating from high school in 1959, she enrolled in Indiana University at Bloomington where she majored in studio art. In 1966 Hahn became interested in photography while studying under Henry Holmes Smith, and stayed on at the University to get her MFA. During that time she worked as Smith's assistant.

In 1967 she moved to Rochester, New York, and worked as a social caseworker until 1969, when she started teaching at the National Technical Institute for the Deaf, located at the Rochester Institute of Technology. After a year she switched to the photography department at R.I.T., teaching advertising photography. In 1976 she received a New York State Council on the Arts grant to pursue her study of non-silver processes and moved to Albuquerque, where she became Associate Professor of Art at the University of New Mexico.

Selected one-woman shows:

1971: Center for Photographic Studies, Louisville, Kentucky

1972: Riverside Studio, Rochester, New York

1973: The Witkin Gallery, New York

1974: Focus Gallery, San Francisco

1976: Nexus Gallery, Atlanta, Georgia
New England School of Photography, Boston

Selected collections:
Museum of Modern Art, New York
George Eastman House, Rochester, New York
Smithsonian Institution, Washington, D.C.
Pasadena Art Museum, Pasadena, California
Art Institute of Chicago
National Gallery of Canada, Ottawa
Akron Art Institute, Akron, Ohio
Virginia Museum of Art, Richmond
University of Kansas Art Museum, Lawrence
University of New Mexico Art Museum, Albuquerque
University of Nebraska Art Museum, Lincoln
Center for Photographic Studies, Louisville, Kentucky
Visual Studies Workshop, Rochester, New York

Alida Cronin

Unlike an invention by a single individual, gum bichromate printing was introduced and reintroduced by a succession of photographers and scientists, each worker adding his own refinements and improvements to the process. In 1852 Fox Talbot patented Photoglyphic Drawing based on the tanning effect of bichromates on a number of organic colloids, including various gums. Alphonse Poitevin modified the process in 1855, and Pouncy patented his results in 1858. Rouillé-Ladevèze announced new findings in 1894, and it was at this time that Robert Demachy and other picture makers adopted this method of printing photographs.

The process gained in popularity among photographers around the turn of the century. Some of the best work of the period was published by Stieglitz in early issues of CAMERA WORK. Gum prints by Demachy, Kühn, Käsebier, Watzek, Hennebert, Puyo, Le Bègue, Steichen, White, and others, appear in the publication from 1903 through 1906. CAMERA WORK issues No. 15 (1906) and No. 21 (1908) include selections of Alvin Langdon Coburn prints that combine the gum bichromate and platinum printing processes.

Gum bichromate (or dichromate) printing is a deceptively easy process. It requires only two chemicals (potassium bichromate and gum arabic) and watercolor pigment and water. It is based on the fact that a bichromated colloid (the gum arabic) becomes insoluble in plain water when exposed to light. While it is essentially a contact printing process of short scale, quite a long range of tones can be built up by multiple printing, if you choose to repeat the sensitizing steps. It offers an unlimited choice of color, an almost unlimited choice in the type of paper or fabric, and personal control of lines, tones, and masses.

Henry Holmes Smith introduced me to the process in 1965. I was looking for a way to print photographs on paper to be bound into a book and was immediately impressed by the fact that the gum solution could be used on etching paper. I was also attracted to the color possibilities and proceeded to experiment with various pigments. Up to this time I had been working in very traditional ways. I had worked with a view camera, had done some of the Zone System tests, shot Tri-X with a Leica, and generally made 8 x 10 enlargements on Agfa paper. The first gum prints I made were this size or smaller, single images of one color. It was the same imagery translated into the color and texture of gum bichromate and very liberating.

Responding to the possibilities of the "new" process was, for me, like changing from a simple declarative sentence, however carefully rendered, to a compound, complex statement of fact and fantasy. The picture was no longer synonymous with the subject because I could manipulate the process and exercise some intellectual control over those details recorded by the camera while incorporating other ideas. Photographic information could be provided where details were included, or it could remain hidden where details were obscured. The quality and quantity of information could be expanded upon as long as the total picture didn't become too cluttered.

Part of the adjustment in imagery included making decisions about the degree of divergence from the camera-made photograph. There were now so many things to consider: the edges, the colors, the multiplication of negatives, the much larger total area, plus the lines, forms, and volumes of the original subjects. Sensual responses to the photograph as object became important to me: how big it was, what kinds of colors there were, how bright or modulated they were, how the paper felt in my hands, how rough or smooth the borders of the photographs were, and how they were handled at the margins.

I also became interested in perceptual responses to images that looked like or didn't look like photographs. I always wanted to deal with those that did look like photographs, and I began to feel that photographic images were highly charged documentary and plastic materials. As long as they retained enough information and detail, photographs could be very malleable. It was possible to use certain areas within them as vacancies or carriers to be filled with relevant details from other sources . . . including the imagination. While protecting that light-rendered look, with delicate handling I could deal with humor or irony or optical illusion or other qualities of thought. The potential for making ordered images out of chaotic ideas seemed limitless.

BALLOON (1968) (Figure 7) represents an attempt to deal with several ideas at the same time. The photographs were made with a Leica while I was working as a social worker. I was concerned about welfare's inability to rescue its recipients from poverty and about what it means to be born poor in a nation of opulence. On another level, I was interested in the perception of images that were repeated but not necessarily in the correct position. Once the figure is established in the viewer's mind, there should be enough repetitious photographic information presented by the left picture to explain the two tipped images on the right. My idea was to upset traditional positioning of photographs without causing the viewer to move his head or turn the picture. The changing color refers to the playful colors of balloons and that compulsion of children to want one after another.

PROCESSED BY KODAK (1968) (Figure 8) is a portrait from the same group as Figure 7 and attempts to deal with several concerns. The metallic silver color in the emulsion plays on the lack of silver in the gum bichromate process, and the sprocket holes allude to that activity for which Kodak is best known. The positioning of the figure in the foreground seeks to establish an ambiguous relationship between what appear to be giant Coke bottles and a normal size man, with the possibility that they might be normal size Cokes in the company of a subminiature man. The lines are obscured and the tones blended together in both the negative and positive versions to support the figure-ground movement. The title is a shameless pun on the thirty years my husband spent at Eastman Kodak.

BROCCOLI (1971) (Figure 9) and CABBAGE (1971) (Figure 10) both come from a later group of Rolleiflex contact prints on paper. Part of a portfolio of twelve images, these prints seek to present a non-aggressive vision with their small scale. The color is carefully mixed to approximate the natural color of the vegetable in each picture. A female torso is used as a pedestal for the vegetable. The single color in each picture exaggerates the vegetable's importance. My intention was to remember the past (the straight photography of Edward Weston, the gum-printed nudes of Demachy, the biological/cultural role of women) but to smile in the present.

PASSPORT PHOTO, BETTY (1970) (Figure 11), is a self-portrait from a group of pictures on fabric that grew out of my musings about the State Department's requirements for travel abroad. The use of photography for keeping track of citizens appealed to me. Police files, grade schools, high schools, and license bureaus must be full of these head shots. Just a small record of the face so one doesn't get mixed up with some other identity. I sought to force a relationship between this untouched and instantaneous photography and the manipulated, time-consuming approach I was using. The negative image obscures rather than clarifies the individual's features, and the stitching emphasizes the person's form rather than personality. The idea of this self-portrait was to reveal very little about myself or my face, but to pay a great deal of attention to the graphic characteristics of the picture—a sort of antithesis to the passport photo.

BROCCOLI (1972) (Figure 12) is from a series of vegetable prints on fabric with color stitching. As with the small vegetables held by the nude, these colors are closely matched to those of the original subject. Unlike the passport photo, these prints represent a conscious effort to clarify the individual features of each organic form, and in that sense they are more specifically portraits than the passport shot. Photographing such common objects allows me to explore the ambiguity of status that occurs when a common object is presented with vivid embellishments—a strange conflict between humility and arrogance. I see most of the stitched pieces as closely related to the figurative stitchery of the nineteenth century. Many of the same sensibilities toward color and subject matter are present.

In order to achieve some of the color and surface results, I made my own modifications in the chemistry. After testing many kinds of paper, I found I was most continuously satisfied with Arches or Rives (etching papers) because both held up when subjected to alternate soaking and drying.

I size the paper in a solution of Knox gelatin to prevent excessive staining by the pigment and potassium. This bath is made by adding two packages of gelatin to a quart of very hot water. The paper remains in the sizing solution for at least five minutes. Excess gelatin is squeegeed off with a glass rod, and the paper is hung on a line to dry. Fabric is sized in a bath of liquid starch (Figure 1)—equal parts starch and water—and dried in the same way.

To mix the sensitizing solution, I use a 10 percent solution of potassium bichromate, staying with small amounts since neither the potassium nor the gum solution keeps for more than a couple of days. Adding ½ oz. dry potassium to 5 oz. warm water makes a convenient amount. This is shielded from light when not in use.

The gum arabic is mixed by adding 5 oz. dry weight to 10 oz. warm water. I use powdered acacia gum arabic, instead of premixed lithographers' gum arabic. It takes several hours to dissolve, but the thicker gum is able to carry more color and yields a darker, richer print. When the two chemicals are completely dissolved, I mix them together using a ratio of 1 part potassium to 3 parts gum.

Color is obtained by adding tube watercolor to the preceding mixture. Exactly how much varies with each color and manufacturer, but a good average is 3 grams of pigment to 2 oz. of the bichromated gum. Winsor & Newton, Pelikan, and Prang watercolors produce the richest tones (Figure 2).

I try to sensitize the paper as quickly and evenly as possible by using long, regular strokes. The more even the coating, the more even the exposure. It is difficult to describe this step of the procedure, but perhaps it would be helpful to know that a lamp black mixture should brush out to look charcoal gray (Figure 3). This can be done in room light, provided there is no direct sun. Drying is done in the dark, and a fan or fan/heater speeds up the process with no side effects. Although the solution for paper and fabric is identical, the drying time for fabric is much longer and it is important that the cloth be thoroughly dry before contact printing.

Large continuous tone negatives can be made by projection printing on Kodalith Ortho or Fine Grain Positive film. I work for a rather high contrast/high density image and control the tonal ranges in the developing (Figure 4). By mixing Kodalith A and B developers with Dektol and water in varying proportions, the contrast can be preserved or altered. A mixture of 1 part A, 1 part B, 1 part Dektol, and 3 parts water will produce a bright, printable negative from a relatively soft

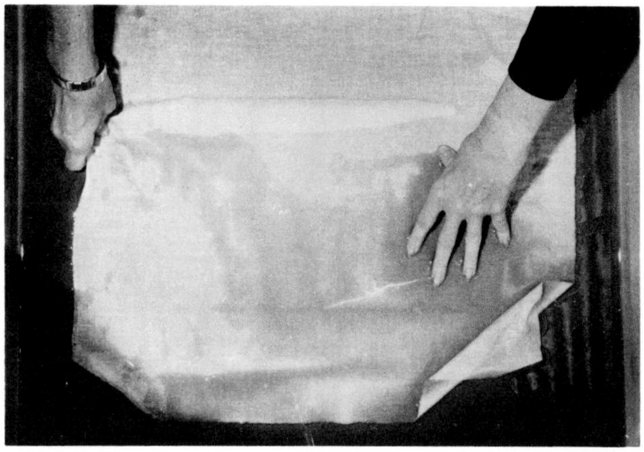

Figure 1.

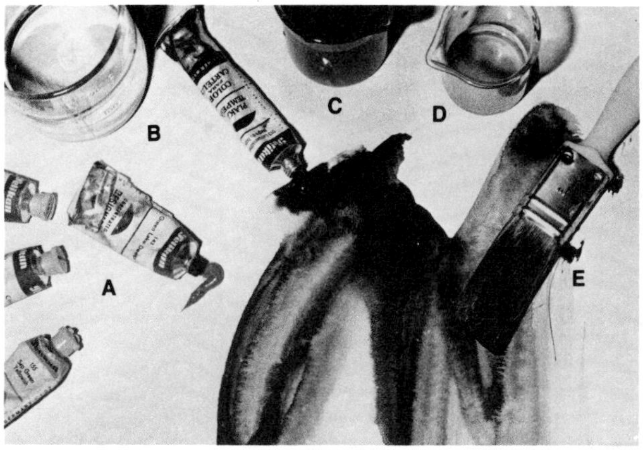

Figure 2.
A: Pigments B: Water C: Potassium bichromate D: Gum arabic (acacia) solution E: Camel hair brush

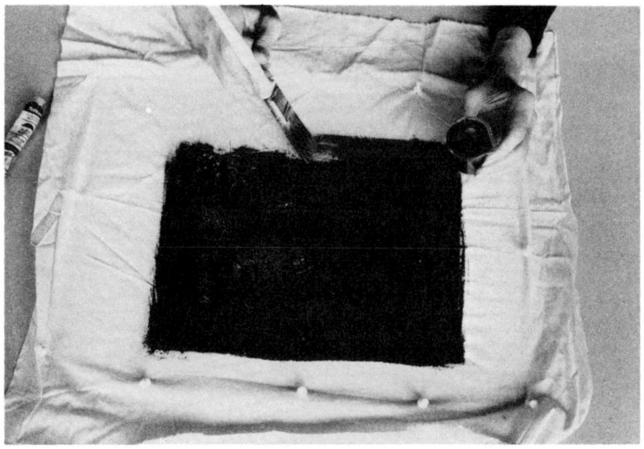

Figure 3.

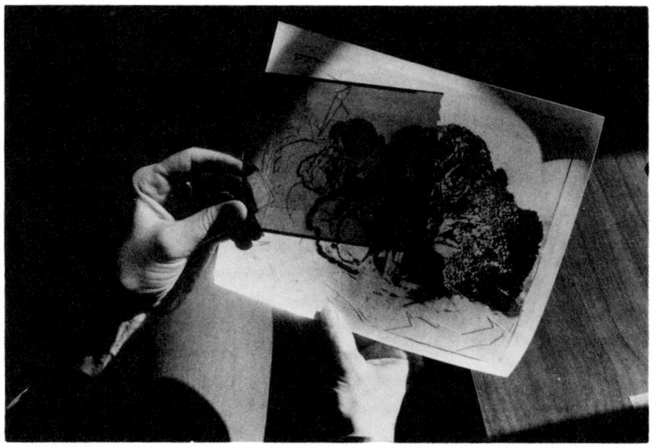

Figure 4.

Figure 5.

Figure 6.

original negative. If I am working with an original negative that is fairly contrasty, I use the same ratio of developers but add 6 or 9 parts water to maintain the middle tones.

The bichromate is hardened by the blue or ultraviolet band of the spectrum, so possible light sources are carbon arc, mercury vapor, sunlight, sunlamps, quartz lights, and photo floods. With the arc lamp that I use, the exposure is eight minutes. With less intense sources of light, the exposure can run as long as thirty minutes.

The print develops in warm water. After about ten minutes in the water, the unexposed areas of the print wash away, leaving only those portions hardened by light. I let the print stay in the water for ten more minutes, until the last traces of potassium have disappeared. Unusually dense areas can be lightened by using a soft brush on them while the print is soaking. A print on fabric will take longer to develop but can survive a much more vigorous brushing to get clean highlights (Figure 5).

To build up a longer range of tones by multiple printing, you must repeat the sensitizing steps. After the print is dry, the gum solution is again applied to the entire surface and reexposed for the same length of time as the first exposure. A system of registry such as holes punched in the margins of the negative is necessary to preserve the detail and focus. Develop and dry as before (Figure 6).

Everyone who has worked with the gum bichromate process seems to adapt it to his or her own picture-making needs, and also makes technical variations suitable to the materials available. The most prolific writer was Robert Demachy. His essays on photography covered technical applications of the gum and bromoil processes as well as aesthetics, criticism, and philosophy.

Published sources of information on gum printing are:

1. Bunnel, Peter C., ed. NONSILVER PRINTING PROCESSES — FOUR SELECTIONS, 1886-1972. Arno Press, New York, 1973.
2. Jay, B. ROBERT DEMACHY. St. Martin's Press, New York, 1974.
3. Clerc, L.P. PHOTOGRAPHY THEORY AND PRACTICE. Pitman Publishing Corp., New York, 1937.
4. Henney, Keith, Dudley, and Beverly, ed. HANDBOOK OF PHOTOGRAPHY. Whittlesley House, New York, 1939.
5. Wall, E.J. PHOTOGRAPHIC FACTS AND FORMULAS. American Publishing Co., Boston, 1940.
6. Kosar, Jaromir. LIGHT SENSITIVE SYSTEMS: CHEMISTRY AND APPLICATION OF NONSILVER HALIDE PHOTOGRAPHIC PROCESSES. Wiley and Sons, Inc., New York, 1965.

FILM	ASA RATING	DEVELOPER	SOLUTION & TIME	AGITATION
Tri-X ——— Kodalith Ortho	Tri-X: 400	Tri-X: Microdol-X ——— 75 F Kodalith A and B ——— 68 F	Microdol-X 1:3 ——— Kodalith A and B Solution A — 1 part Solution B — 1 part Dektol — 1 part water — 3 parts	Tri-X: 5 seconds in every 30 seconds ——— Kodalith: in tank, rock in circular motion ——— In tray, continuously

ENLARGER	LENS	LIGHT SOURCE	USUAL APERTURE	USUAL EXPOSURE
Omega D2V	Componar-C 50mm *f*/3.5 ——— Componar-C 75mm *f*/4	No. 212	*f*/8	10 to 12 seconds

PAPER	DEVELOPER	SOLUTION & TIME	STOP BATH	FIXER
Rives or Arches etching paper ——— 100% cotton fabric	Water ——— 75 F	Paper: 5 to 10 minutes ——— Fabric: 15 minutes	None	None

WASH	TONING	DRYING	FLATTENING	PRESENTATION
None	None	For paper and fabric: air dry on fresh blotters	Paper: None ——— Fabric: sprayed with water and ironed on reverse side ——— Set iron to "cotton" setting or medium high	Paper: "float" mounted in hinged, all rag mattes ——— Fabric: wrapped around 4-ply rag board, rag taped ——— Under glass

Figure 7: BALLOON, gum bichromate on Rives paper with applied color

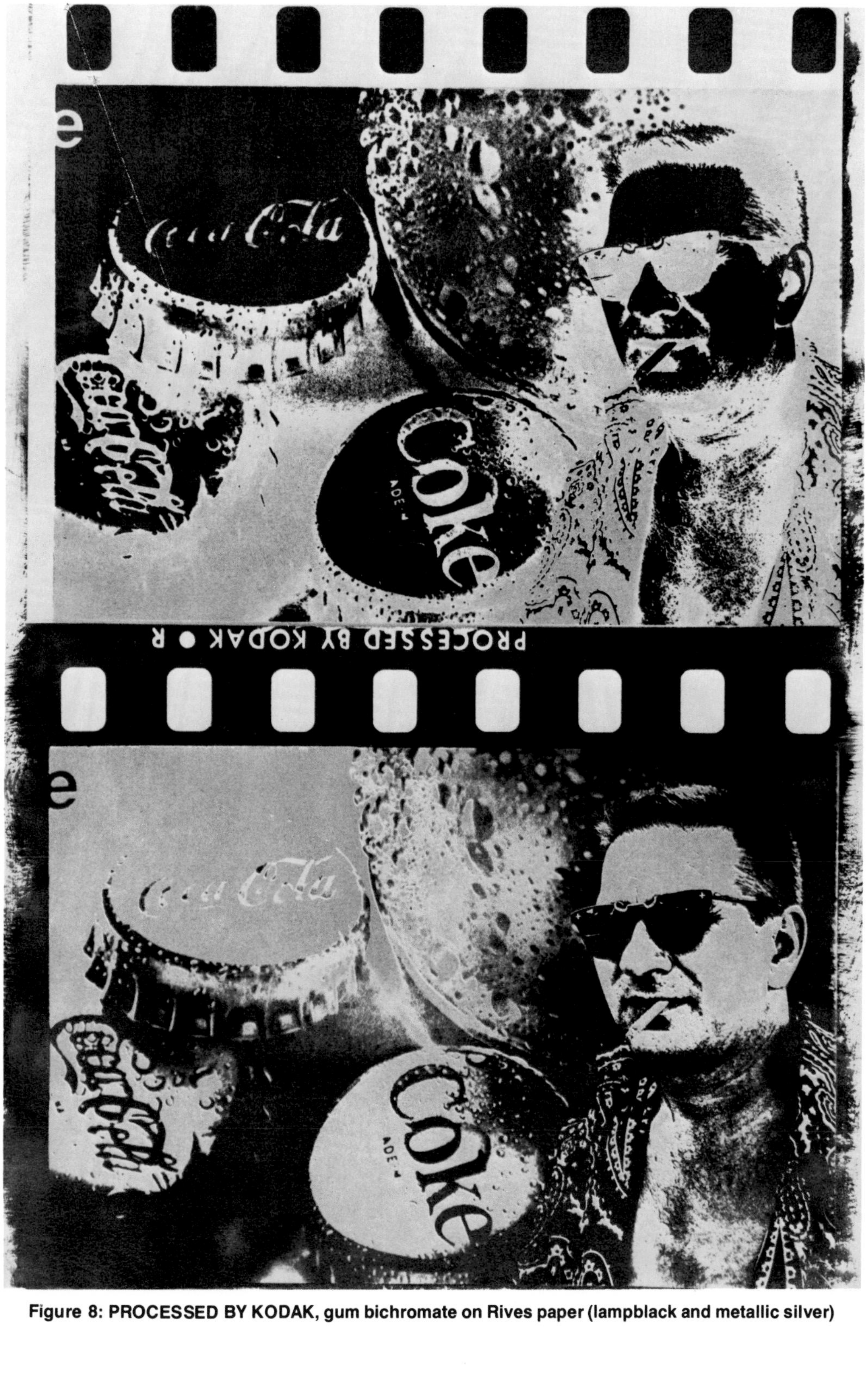

Figure 8: PROCESSED BY KODAK, gum bichromate on Rives paper (lampblack and metallic silver)

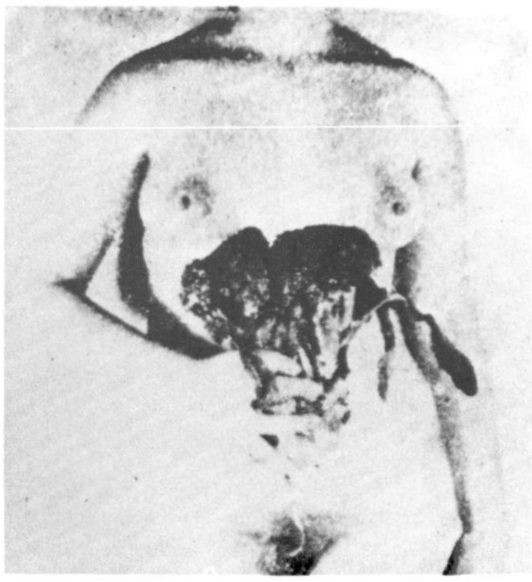

Figure 9: BROCCOLI
gum bichromate on Rives paper

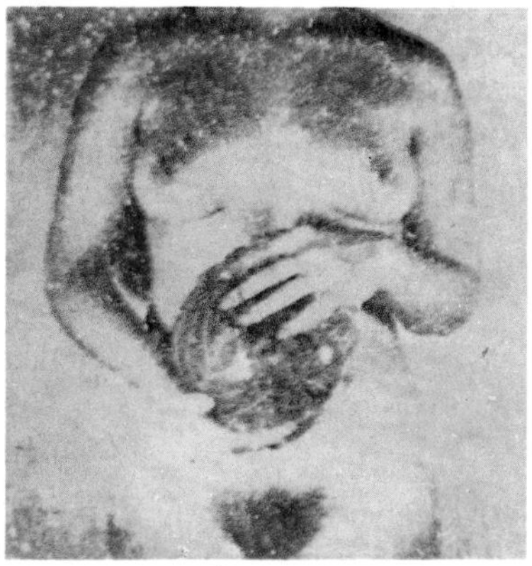

Figure 10: CABBAGE
gum bichromate on Rives paper

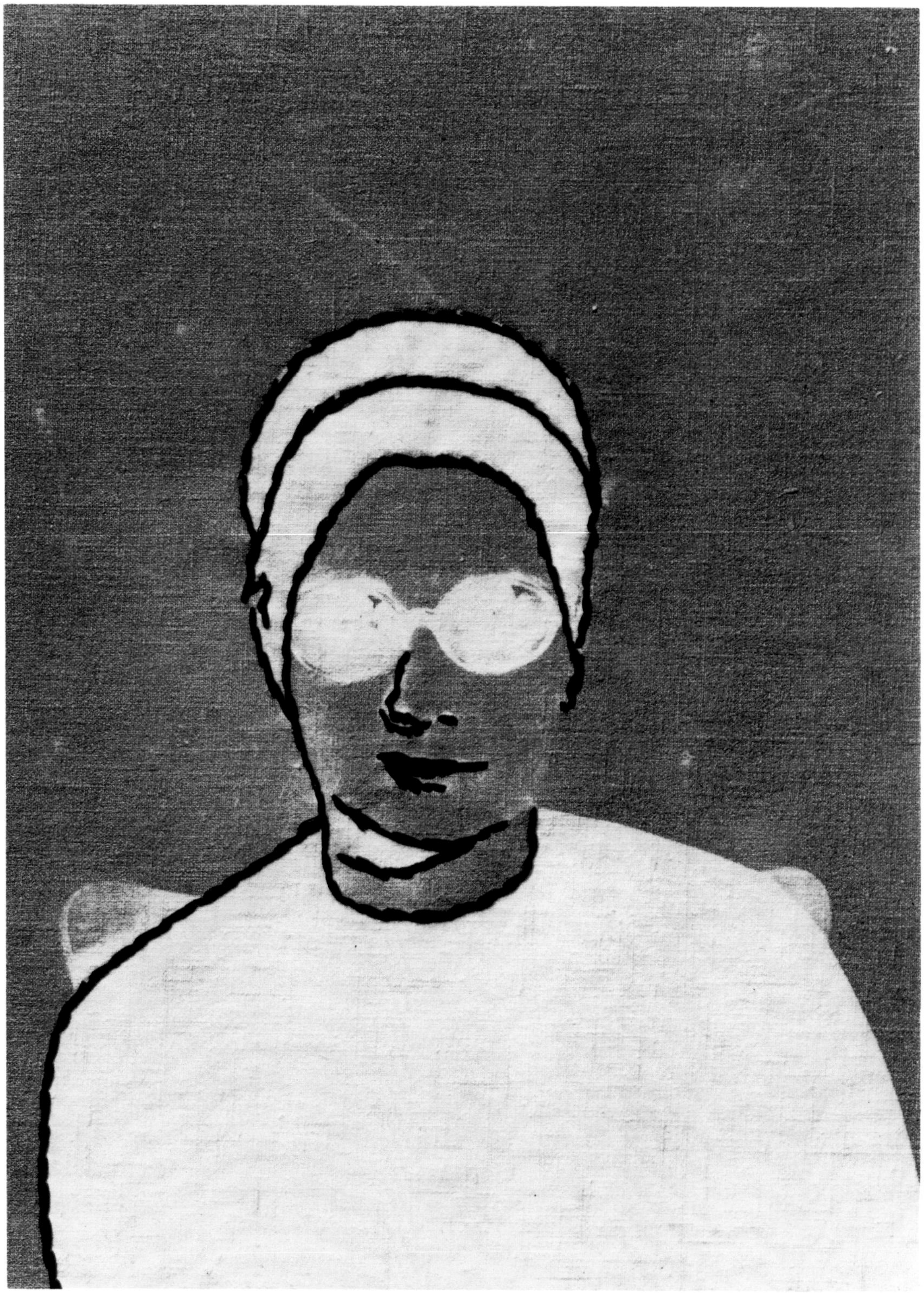

Figure 11: PASSPORT PHOTO, BETTY, gum bichromate on cotton/dacron (metallic silver) with stitching

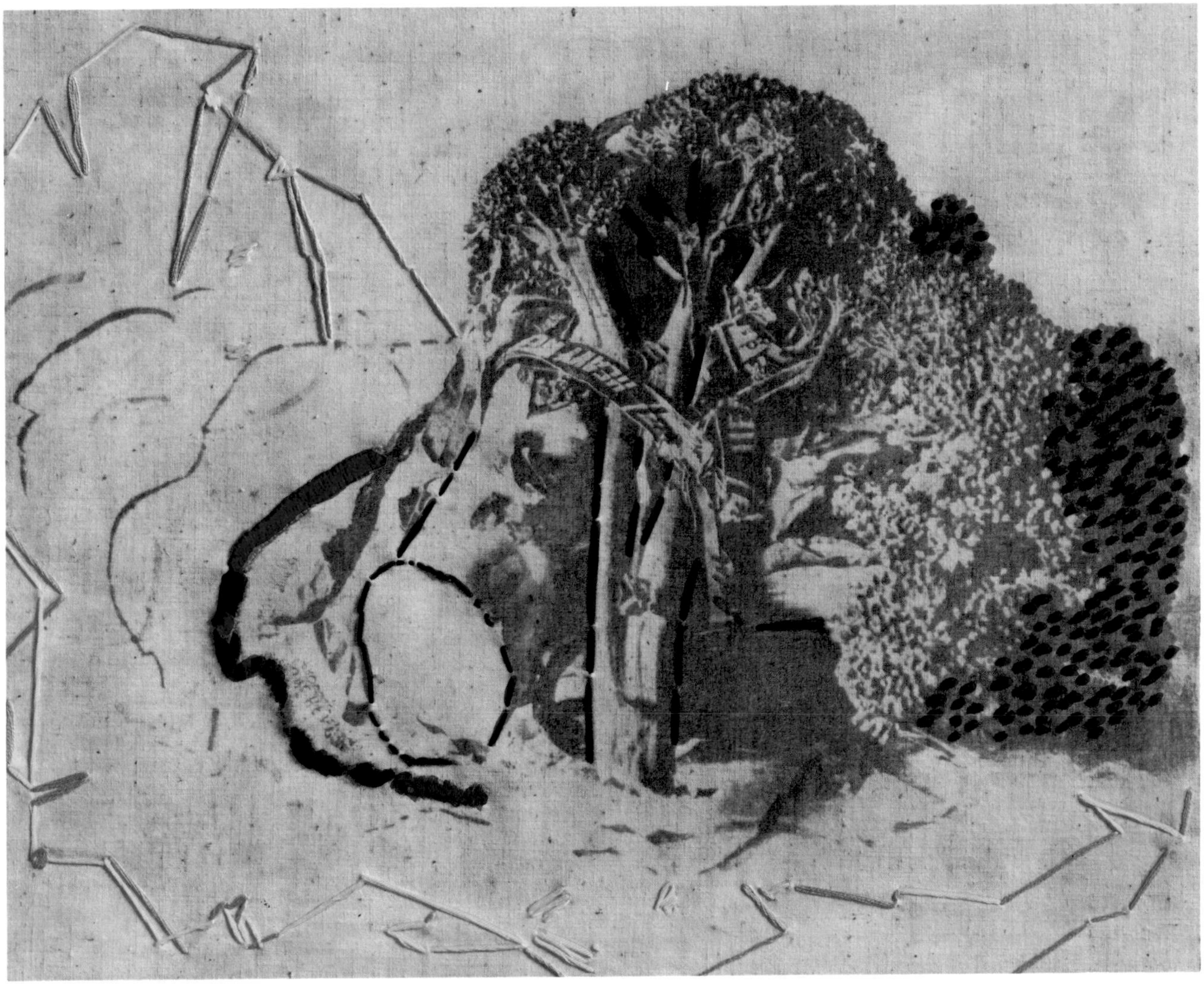

Figure 12: BROCCOLI, gum bichromate on muslin with added stitching

EIKOH HOSOE

Eikoh Hosoe was born in Yonezawa City, Yamagata prefecture in 1933. He grew up in Tokyo. In 1950 he won the grand prize in the student section of the Fuji Film contest and went on to study photography at the Tokyo College of Photography. After graduation in 1954, he became a free-lance photographer and, in 1959, organized a group called Vivo with Shomei Tomatsu and others.

In 1960 Hosoe made a film, NAVAL AND ATOMIC BOMB, and won the Most Promising Photographer Award of the Japan Photo Critics Association. His first book, MAN AND WOMAN (Camerart, Tokyo), appeared in 1961, followed by KILLED BY ROSES (Shuei-sha, Tokyo) in 1963. He directed two sections of the Tokyo Olympics film in 1964. Hosoe continues to produce books—KAMAITACHI (Gendarshicho-sha, Tokyo) in 1969, EMBRACE (Shashinhyoronsha, Tokyo) in 1970, ORDEAL BY ROSES (Shuei-sha, Tokyo) in 1971, as well as children's books in English, such as WHY, MOTHER, WHY? (Kodansha International, Tokyo) in 1965. TAKACHAN AND I (Norton, New York) was published in 1967 and RETURN TO HIROSHIMA (Atheneum, New York) in 1969. In 1970, Hosoe received the Minister of Education Award of the Arts.

He teaches at the Tokyo College of Photography.

Selected one-man shows outside Japan:

1969: Smithsonian Institution, Washington, D.C.
1970: Phoenix College, Phoenix, Arizona
1972: Visual Studies Workshop, Rochester, New York
1973: Light Gallery, New York
1974: Foto and Film Centrum, Antwerp, Belgium
1975: Light Gallery, New York
1976: University of Arizona, Tucson

Selected collections:
The Museum of Modern Art, Tokyo
George Eastman House, Rochester, New York
Museum of Modern Art, New York
Smithsonian Institution, Washington, D.C.
Yale University Art Museum, New Haven, Connecticut
National Gallery of Canada, Ottawa
Bibliothèque Nationale, Paris

With the photo that decided my future

Figure 1.

The darkroom is a place to think, a sort of workshop (Figure 1). It is a resting place. I think back to the image I photographed, and I work to create something out of that remembered image. Sometimes my effort is to match the image I photographed. Sometimes, something new is created. I make discoveries in the darkroom. While printing, I may get an unexpected effect. If it seems right to me, I make it mine. I think about my photographs while I am in the darkness.

My darkroom technique is very simple. I use Tri-X and Plus-X because I know their characteristics. My developing is done with D-76 according to the directions at 20 degrees C (68 degrees F) for six to ten minutes. I cut developing time 10 to 15 percent. My negatives are comparatively thin, but they retain detail in the shadow areas. If an exposure is well made, you can get a beautiful shadow area. Mine is sort of a Zone System. I'm not aware of the Zone System scientifically, but I think every photographer has his own form of Zone System without being conscious of it.

I make many prints before I get my final one. Sometimes it takes an hour and sometimes a whole week. I work for the delicate details in the shadow area. I'm concerned about this area because it is mysterious. There is an obscure world in the darkness. I don't feel much for the highlight but I respect it and treat it so that the whiteness may not seem the whiteness of the paper, but the whiteness of the thing itself. I print for the shadows first and then burn in the rest of the image. Mine is an additive process.

I prefer to use high contrast paper and a rather thin negative to low contrast paper with a dense negative. I use all kinds of photographic papers — the Japanese papers Gekko and Fuji Bromide, also Brovira III and Ilfomar III. For reproduction purposes I use single weight glossy paper. With it you can get a clearer white and more details in the shadows. The glossy surface widens the tonal range and is well suited for copying. Moreover, single weight paper can be easily handled in the darkroom because it needs less washing time. For shows I use a variety of papers, depending on the images. If you respect the details of your imagery, you will find the appropriate paper.

Burning and dodging are both strong weapons. By using them I can alter the original image and refine it. The negative shows everything. It's raw. You must cook it. At the moment of taking the picture, I think of preparing it in the "kitchen." To dodge, I use cutout forms—circles, squares, irregular shapes attached to an eight-inch piece of piano wire (Figure 2). I dance around with these shapes. For burning in, I use regular photographic paper with all kinds of holes cut in it (Figure 3). One side of my paper is black and one side white, so that when the negative is so dark I can't see where the light is going, I use the white side of the paper and see the

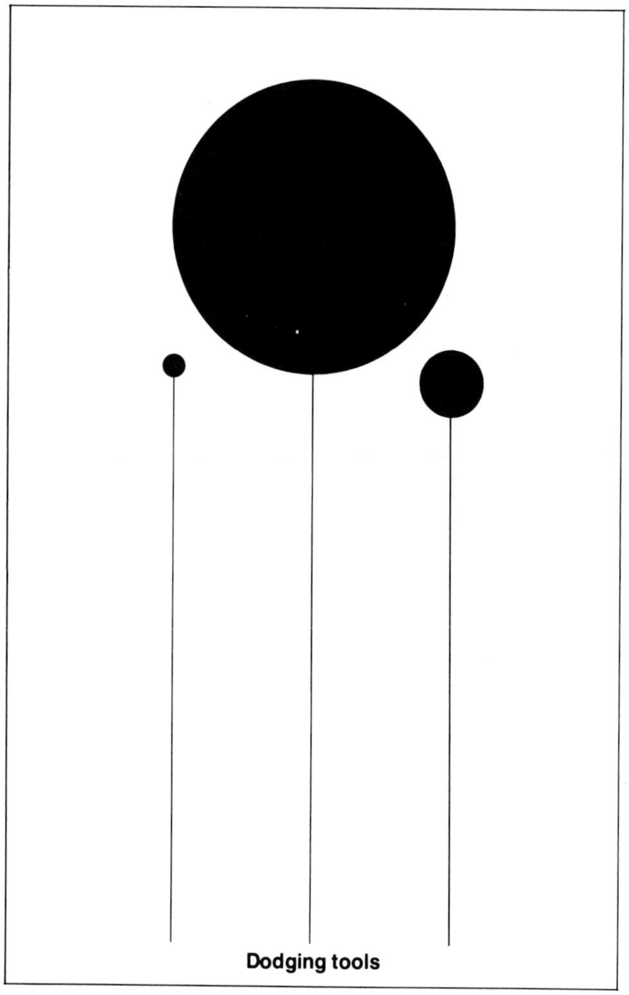

Figure 2.

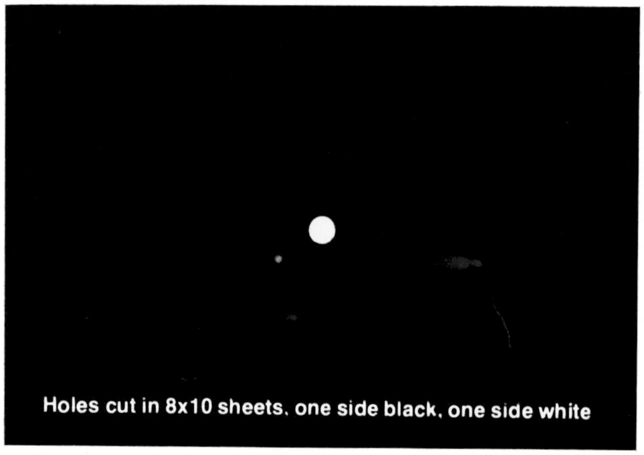

Holes cut in 8x10 sheets, one side black, one side white

Figure 3.

image on it. I also use my hands.

The paper developers I use are Ilfophen and Gekkol (Mitsubishi Paper Company). With these developers, each photographic paper has its recommended developing time. With Brovira I develop the print from one and a half to two and a half minutes. With Ilfomar, two minutes. And with Gekko paper, three minutes or more.

After the stop bath, I use two hypo baths. Then I wash just a single print at a time in ten changes of water. Then a solution of Quick Wash (Fuji Film Company), a hypo-clearing agent, and wash the print again in ten more changes of water. It takes much time.

Sometimes I'm tempted to make non-permanent prints, prints that change color, fade away. I think about a show of prints that would disappear in ten days. This is another characteristic of photography. People are so concerned with the archival process. We believe that prints should last more than a hundred years, but wouldn't it be wonderful to make ephemeral prints? I wouldn't do it now because I am too much concerned with the preservation of prints.

For exhibition prints I use air drying shelves. There is a stack of ten over the ferrotyping machine where the heat reaches them indirectly. Afterwards I place a print between acid-free blotters and press it in a dry mount press at low heat for three to five minutes. Sometimes I flatten a print under a heavy weight. That takes a day or so.

I use mostly the Nikon F or the Nikkormat, but own many old cameras because I love them. I have a Deardorf 8 x 10, a Deardorf 5 x 7 with a 4 x 5 back, and a Sinar 8 x 10. For the Deardorf, a handmade camera, I have obtained a handmade lens, a Goertz Dagor, and I'm looking for a handmade tripod. I also have an Olympus Pen, a Mamiya RB 67, and an Asahi Pentax, both with a 6 x 7 cm (2¼ x 2¾) format, and a Rolleiflex with a 6 x 6 cm (2¼ x 2¼) format.

The first two photographs (Figures 5 and 6) are from the book KILLED BY ROSES that I did of Yukio Mishima, the novelist. This project came together by chance. Mr. Mishima asked me to take pictures of him for one of his books. Interested in photographing him more, I asked him to become my model and began photographing him frequently.

About a year later I wanted to make a book using these pictures. Mr. Mishima hesitated at first. But I insisted, convincing him that this was a worthwhile project since it would present a book of photographs of him for the first time.

We went with the publisher to a Japanese-style hotel where we had rented a big room, a completely open space. I spread out the huge enlargements I had made of my photographs. The publisher was enthusiastic about using these pictures at the exact size I had printed them, as I had hoped he would be. Thus the format of KILLED BY ROSES became the straight enlargement from 35mm, narrow and vertical.

I asked Mr. Mishima to make a title for the book and he sent me a list of about ten. I liked ORDEAL BY ROSES very much. KILLED BY ROSES is a misinterpretation of the original title, but we liked it, so it became the first English title.

When the book was reedited, Mr. Mishima asked me to change the title to ORDEAL BY ROSES. Maybe he didn't like the word "killed." (I think this was significant in light of his subsequent suicide.) I agreed, since "ordeal" was closer to the original Japanese meaning. I also had a feeling that I wanted to change the book itself. So I asked the designer, Tadanori Yokoo, to join us in building a new work. I did the sequencing of photographs and he designed the format, the book cover, and added a new chapter, with his illustrations and my new photographs. The book became ORDEAL BY ROSES.

The portrait of Mr. Mishima (Figure 5) from KILLED BY ROSES was shot on microfilm, Fuji minicopy film. Everybody says that I make contrasty pictures by using microfilm, but this is the first and last time I ever used it. I chose microfilm in order to obtain high contrast with shadow details at the same time. To get this detail, I rated the film at 10 although the original ASA is 32. Then I developed it for 50 percent less than normal time in D-76. I wanted the powerful effect of the contrast to show Mr. Mishima's strength.

Since all the prints in the book were for reproduction, I used the Japanese paper Gekko V 2, 3, and 4, glossy. It is very good for my work because it brings out details in the dark areas. You can push the paper for four minutes or more without fogging it and get beautiful tonal gradation.

The picture of THE COUPLE (Figure 6) from KILLED BY ROSES was shot on Tri-X, as was the rest of the book. It was taken at a friend's dance studio. He has a tiny balcony-like room overlooking the studio below. I shot from the door to this room, leaning out over the studio while someone held onto my legs. The exposure was *f*/11 at ¼ second. I used two photofloods for lighting, one on the side and one shining from the ceiling. I placed a painted canvas on the floor and had the couple lie on it. In the negative the edge of the canvas shows clearly (Figure 7). I did not want this, but it was difficult to eliminate in the shooting. I could not underexpose because the negative would have become too thin. While shooting, I realized that this canvas edge could be burned in when I printed the negative.

The removal of spatial clues by burning in tends to create a graphic flatness. I see perspective and distance in this flatness. We Japanese are accustomed to looking at paintings or woodblock prints that have such a perspective. We see distance, mood and layers of air in this flatness. I have that traditional sense in my photographs.

The photograph of KNEES (Figure 8) is from an exhibition

NELSON GOLD TONER
(E.K. Co., US Patent No. 1,849,245)

Solution A:
water, 125 F — 1 gallon
sodium thiosulfate (hypo) — 2 pounds
ammonium persulfate — 4 ounces

Dissolve hypo before adding persulfate. Stir while adding persulfate. Bath should turn milky. Increase temperature until it does. Prepare the following solution and add it to the mixture above. Stir vigorously. Bath must be cool when mixing these solutions.
cold water — 2 ounces
silver nitrate — 75 grains
(silver nitrate must be completely
dissolved before adding sodium chloride)
sodium chloride — 75 grains

Solution B:
water — 8 ounces
gold chloride — 15 grains
(gold chloride is supplied in 15 grain glass containers)

Add 4 ounces of Solution B to the entire quantity of Solution A, stirring vigorously. Do not use until bath has become cold and forms a sediment. Pour off the sediment. Clear solution is poured into a tray supported by a hot water bath, heated to 110 F. Temperature should be 110 F during toning process. Dry prints should be thoroughly soaked before toning. Wet prints should be washed and fixed before toning.

When desired tone has been reached, remove from tray and rinse in cold water. After all prints have been toned, return to fixing bath for 5 minutes, then wash for 1 hour. Bath is revived by the addition of gold Solution B. When toning to warm brown, add 4cc after each 50 8x10 prints (or equivalent) have been toned. Keep solution to proper volume. Add more as needed.

Figure 4.

on the nude that I called EMBRACE. These photographs later came out as a book. For this series I used Plus-X because of the finer grain and rendition of detail. It has more contrast than Tri-X, which I wanted in order to emphasize the differences in skin tone of the man and woman. In the darkroom I continued to exaggerate this effect. I knew that it would be impossible to create directly from the negative, so I sensed dodging and burning while shooting. Technique does not exist independently. It comes from the original idea. The images spring from traditional Japanese art in the sense that the female is always white and the male dark. Even nowadays, women use white powder. This whiteness is still woman's desire and man's desire too. Here the whiteness is that of the paper itself, but I feel that it is the whiteness of skin, the whiteness of the female, female itself.

The photographs for this series were shot with the Nikon F and the 55mm Micro-Nikkor and 85mm *f*/1.8 lenses. The image of the knees was made with the Micro-Nikkor.

For the EMBRACE exhibition, I used Japanese Eagle paper. I tested and tested and found that Eagle was best for these images because I could obtain a beautiful gold toning effect with it. Gold toning is good to preserve the print, but the archival effect is a by-product for me here. I did it for aesthetic reasons, using the Nelson Gold Tone process (Figure 4), which is a very old process, a classic.

After fixing the print, place it in the gold toning bath. It's at 110 F. So we call it a hot spring. Soak the print in the bath and watch the effect. When satisfied, take it out and rinse it in cold water. This stops the process. Then put the print in hypo again, and wash it. I left these prints in the toner for about five minutes.

When I have a show, I take plenty of time to decide on the size of the prints. In the darkroom, I try different sizes from 4 x 5 to 16 x 20. Then I can see the effect and decide. For EMBRACE, the print has to be either very small or very large. If small, you can sense it as one of your personal belongings. If it's big, projected on a wall, it's very strong. (I have a plan to project this image on an empty white wall in Tokyo.) But if it's somewhere in between, the strength of the flesh, the spirit of the flesh is reduced.

With this series I had a desire to restore the spirit of the flesh to the physical flesh. These days, people don't respect the body. They think that the head is almighty. But the body has its own spirit, and when the physical and the spiritual are combined, it's ideal. In the series I wanted to emphasize this, so I carefully left out the heads, the faces, so you may feel that this could be you or anybody else. The figures aren't Japanese or American or French.. They are universal.

The last two images are from my show at the Light Gallery in New York called SIMON, A PRIVATE LANDSCAPE. This is based on the memory of my life after the war, about 1950 or so. It is a continuation of the previous series KAMAITACHI, which was based on the memory of my childhood during the war when I was evacuated to the country and separated from my family. The atmosphere of this new series is that of a strange mood without significance. It is difficult to record memory using the medium of photography, so I always need a catalyst. Here, Simon becomes the catalyst. Sometimes this kind of man was inside me. He exists in this landscape as an apparition. Sometimes he fades away. Every image has meaning, although I say it's a landscape with no significance. This field is a place where I used to play as a child. This flower grew near my house after the war. I wanted to record it even though it appalls me. It seems foreign. I hate its dusty yellow pollen. It is a forbidden flower, and since it is forbidden, I want to touch it. There is an ambivalence in Simon's gesture, something awful about it. It is a sad image. These images from SIMON, A PRIVATE LANDSCAPE are absolutely personal. I did not think of people's reaction to them. The images are open to interpretation.

For these photographs I used Tri-X developed in D-76. The image of SIMON WITH THE FLOWER (Figure 9) was shot with the Micro-Nikkor 55mm at *f*/5.6 at 1/125. This is my standard lens, rather than the 50mm *f*/1.4. I can photograph any object with it, from right in front of my eyes into the distant mountains, moons, and stars. It is almighty.

For the image of SIMON IN THE FIELD (Figure 10), I wanted full detail in the grass and in his face, so I used the Sinar with a Fuji 75mm lens at *f*/16 for 1/4. This is a super-wide-angle lens when used with a 4 x 5 format.

I tried many papers and found that this series required Ilfomar III. The black is a little warm, and that warmth was the best suited for these images. The developer is Gekkol. I also gold toned the paper for about thirty seconds for archival purposes and to warm the print tone slightly.

Here again the size of the prints is important. After much trial and error I decided on the image size 30 x 40 cm (12 x 16). This size is perfect for the nature of the images in relation to the size of the gallery, its scale and the color of the background. In my studio, I tested the size and sequencing of the prints on the floor. I thought about how they would look in the gallery and was satisfied.

Generally I make a larger print when working with 35mm negatives and a smaller or contact print from large format negatives like 4 x 5 or 8 x 10. I believe, however, that print size is decided by the image itself. Ask your photographs to decide the size of the print.

FILM	ASA RATING	DEVELOPER	SOLUTION & TIME	AGITATION
Tri-X Plus-X Fuji Neopan SSS	Varies	D-76 Konidal Super (Tri-X at ASA 800) 68 F	Varies	Continuous for first minute, then 5 seconds in every 30 seconds

ENLARGER	LENS	LIGHT SOURCE	USUAL APERTURE	USUAL EXPOSURE
Focomat 1C Nikon Omega D2	EL-Nikkor 50mm *f*/2.8 EL-Nikkor 35mm *f*/5.6 EL-Nikkor 80mm *f*/5.6	No. 212	2 stops down	Varies

PAPER	DEVELOPER	SOLUTION & TIME	STOP BATH	FIXER
Brovira III Ilfomar III Gekko All grades	Gekkol Ilfophen	Solution varies Time varies	28% glacial acetic acid solution 15 to 30 seconds	Fuji Fix 2 baths 3½ minutes in each

WASH	TONING	DRYING	FLATTENING	PRESENTATION
Each print gets 10 changes of water*	Selenium GP-1 (Nelson Gold Toner, Page 95)	Air dry on fiberglass screen	Sandwiched between fresh blotters in drymount press for 5 minutes at low temperature	Drymount on museum board Frame with overmatte, under glass

*Single weight prints: 30 seconds, running water, 2 minutes Quick Wash, 10 minutes in running water, final wash. Double weight prints: 1 minute, running water, 6 minutes Quick Wash, 12 minutes in running water, final wash.

Figure 5: PORTRAIT OF YUKIO MISHIMA

Figure 6: THE COUPLE

Figure 7: THE COUPLE

Figure 8: KNEES

Figure 9: SIMON WITH THE FLOWER

Figure 10: SIMON IN THE FIELD

GEORGE KRAUSE

George Krause was born in Philadelphia in 1937. He studied at the Philadelphia College of Art and began photographing in 1957, while in the Army.

He returned to the Philadelphia College of Art in 1959 to study photography and worked on QUI RIPOSA, a series of photographs of Italian-American gravestones. In 1963 he received a Fulbright grant to photograph in Spain. By 1964 he had begun SAINTS AND MARTYRS, a complementary series to QUI RIPOSA dealing with Indo-Hispanic statues in Central and South American churches.

Krause returned to Spain in 1967 on a Guggenheim Fellowship. Two years later he received a Philadelphia College of Art Alumni grant.

GEORGE KRAUSE I (Toll and Armstrong, Haverford, Pennsylvania) was published in 1972. In 1976 he received his second Guggenheim Fellowship and became the first photographer to win the Prix de Rome Fellowship.

On his return from Rome in 1977, he resumes his position as Assistant Professor of Art at the University of Houston where he has been developing a photography program.

Selected one-man shows:

1970: Museo de Bellas Artes, Caracas, Venezuela

1972: The Photographer's Place, Philadelphia, Pennsylvania

1974: Photopia Gallery, Philadelphia, Pennsylvania

1975: The Print Club, Philadelphia, Pennsylvania

1976: Photopia Gallery, Philadelphia, Pennsylvania
Enjay Gallery, Boston, Massachusetts
Afterimage, Dallas, Texas

1977: Houston Museum of Fine Arts, Houston, Texas

Selected collections:
Museum of Modern Art, New York
George Eastman House, Rochester, New York
Philadelphia Art Museum, Philadelphia, Pennsylvania
New York Public Library
Library of Congress, Washington, D.C.
Bibliothèque Nationale, Paris
Fogg Art Museum, Cambridge, Massachusetts

Nancy Crampton

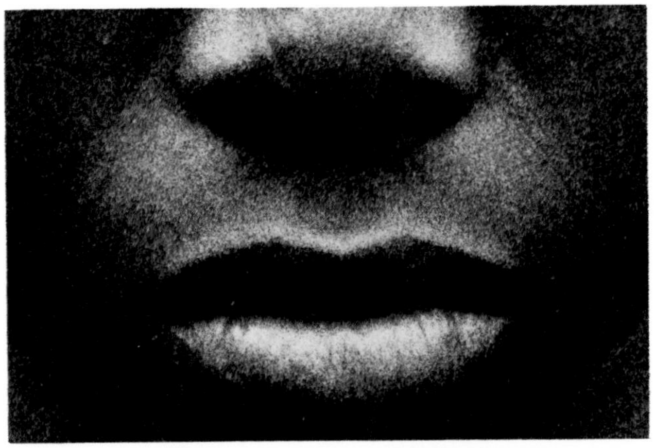

Figure 1: Fragment of THE SCAR

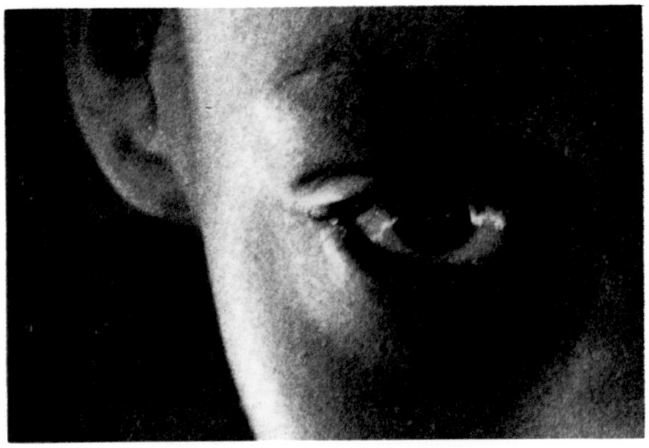

Figure 2: Fragment of BLACK BOY

As a photography student back in the late fifties, I fell in love with a beautiful photographic enlarging paper called Kodak Illustrators Special. Its surface and tone were perfect as far as I was concerned. I hoped one day, when I could afford it, to gold tone this paper. In the meantime I was very happy with the results obtained using selenium toner. There was only one problem with this paper. It was limited to a fixed grade of contrast of about two and one-half. At the time, my technique was a bit clumsy, and since I could not and would not give up this beautiful paper, I had to adapt my negatives to match the fixed contrast of my Illustrators Special. (Kodak Ektalure is similar but not quite as beautiful.) In frustration, I tried everything. I experimented with many different types of intensifiers, but always ended with a grain pattern that is generally referred to as "marbles." Once I broke down and cried when a chromium intensifier butchered a negative, and felt better only after I destroyed the ruined negative.

I had to find a better way. It all began in a somewhat vague and dreamlike manner. I recall walking into a small, seedy photography shop and explaining my problem to the proprietor. He nodded knowingly and went into the back room. After a few minutes he reappeared holding a small glass vial. "Just follow the instructions and everything will be fine," he said. I did, and it was. I had discovered Victor's Mercury Intensifier (hereafter referred to as VMI).

It is generally assumed that we use intensification only when an error has occurred, either in exposure or development. Usually this mistake results in a thin, flat negative that will not even yield a print of decent contrast on a No. 6 enlarging paper. The negative is thrown into something known as an intensifier only as a last resort. Actually, dense flat negatives caused either by overexposure, overdevelopment, or both can also be improved with the use of VMI. The grain structure of these dense negatives is confused and mushy. VMI can increase the contrast, relieving the flatness. It will also arrange the grain structure in an interesting pointillist pattern (Figure 1), particularly noticeable when working with a dense flat negative.

I have also intensified negatives of normal density to either change the grain pattern or give more tonal separation (Figure 2). Early in my career, I earned a living by printing the intaglio (etchings and engravings, etc.) work of successful artists. I believe this had an effect on some of my earliest work, especially the dark prints I loved to make and still do. Black detail in a dark background is very exciting to me. Detail that normally would be lost in the dark areas is made more visible with VMI. The VMI intensification process adapts the photographic grain pattern of either the dense or thin flat negative into a pattern that resembles aquatint or fine mezzotint. This grain pattern also reminds me of the texture of some of Seurat's drawings.

The VMI instructions used to suggest that all film be processed in whatever developer you use but for a slightly shorter time than usual; then it should be fixed, washed, and finally immersed in VMI for a minute or so. I would not go quite that far. Blindly intensifying all negatives seems to me a technical and aesthetic crutch. I recommend first making as good a print as possible using filters or high contrast enlarging paper. Some people suggest making a duplicate negative and intensifying it rather than risking damage to the original. Only after I had determined that I could never obtain the contrast or effect I wanted through printing would I use VMI or another appropriate intensifier.

There are many different kinds of intensifiers. There is even a method of intensification of the latent image. It sounds rather complicated, and since I have not experimented with it, I will not discuss this technique except to mention it. I've come across at least fifteen intensifiers, including uranium, silver, copper, chromium, Monckhoven's quinone-thiosulfate, lead, and many other mercuric chloride and mercuric iodide intensifiers. These are divided into three separate families. First, there are those intensifiers that just increase contrast by attacking the densest areas of the negative. Second are the proportional intensifiers, which increase equally the densities of the entire negative. The third group of intensifiers is designed to work mainly on the thin, weak areas of the negative. VMI's properties strengthen detail especially in the thin, weak areas, create greater separation of tone, and of course, increase contrast. For a comparison of other intensifiers to VMI, see Figure 3.

The use of VMI has a risk factor since it is necessary to wet and soften the emulsion prior to intensification, making it vulnerable to scratching, etc. But using most of the other intensifiers involves even greater risk, without increased benefit. The intensification cannot be reversed with the ones that bleach first and redevelop. With VMI, the negative may be returned to its original state by immersing it in hypo.

Alas, VMI is no longer manufactured. Since the formula was a secret, I had to discover for myself the ingredients and proportions that made up this amazing compound. I decided to call the Smith-Victor Company, which had manufactured it. I wanted to know if there was any other information regarding VMI that they would send me, and why they had stopped production. I spoke with a Mr. Smith, who told me there were two main reasons for discontinuing VMI. The first was a drop in sales. I suspect it never was a very popular product. If VMI had been promoted as extensively as some of the chromium intensifiers, for example, I feel it would have been more commercially successful. I've met only a few photographers who had ever heard of VMI. Everyone I've introduced it to has been impressed with the results. The second reason Smith-Victor gave up producing it was the toxic nature of its components. No company can afford to meet the government safety standards required to manufacture such a dangerous compound. I was surprised when Mr. Smith offered to send me the no longer secret formula. All those photographers who had already discovered VMI on their own and had wondered how to obtain more, can now make it themselves. With thanks to the Smith-Victor Company, here is the formula for Victor's Mercury Intensifier.

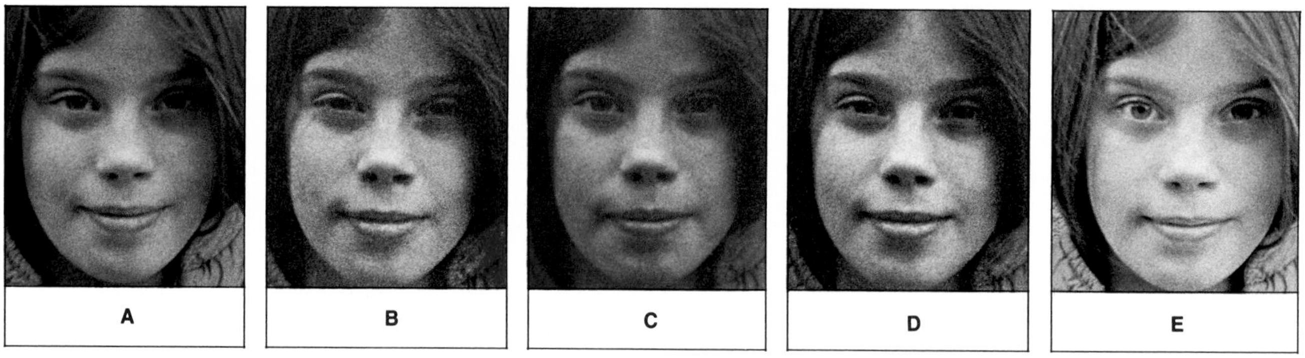

Figure 3: This comparison test was made with Ilford's HP4 film. Half the roll was purposely overexposed and the other half, underexposed. The film was underdeveloped in D-76, diluted 1:1, to produce a roll of flat negatives. All the prints were developed in full strength Dektol to reveal a more pronounced grain pattern. The first illustration (A) is of a thin negative printed on No. 6 paper. The next print (B) is made from a thin flat negative that has been intensified with a copper intensifier for 10 minutes and printed on variable contrast paper, printed with a No. 3 filter. Another thin flat negative was intensified with chromium intensifier (C). The negative was bleached, cleared and redeveloped twice and then printed on variable contrast paper with a No. 4 filter. The last two illustrations (D and E) are of negatives that have been intensified with VMI. (D) is from a thin flat negative while (E) is from a dense flat negative. Both were printed on variable contrast paper with a No. 3 filter.

mercuric chloride NF powder — 1¾ oz.
magnesium sulfate, purified dried powder — 8 oz.
potassium iodide USP granular — 4 oz.
sodium sulfite, anhydrous photo (desiccated) — 2 oz.
water to make one gallon

Stir to thoroughly dissolve the ingredients in water at approximately 70 F. (If you decide to make a quart or half gallon, divide the formula accordingly.) Allow the solution to stand for a few minutes. A yellow precipitate will sink to the bottom. Pour off the clear liquid from the mixing graduate into a dark or opaque container. Use of a filter to exclude the precipitate is a good idea but not absolutely necessary. Store in a dark place until ready to use, since mercuric chloride is unstable when exposed to light.

THIS SOLUTION IS EXTREMELY POISONOUS AND MUST NOT BE TAKEN INTERNALLY. IF IT HAPPENS BY ACCIDENT, VOMITING MUST BE INDUCED AS QUICKLY AS POSSIBLE. THE CONTAINER SHOULD BE CLEARLY MARKED AND STORED AWAY FROM CHILDREN. USE SURGICAL GLOVES WHEN IN CONTACT WITH THE SOLUTION.

The chemicals used in the formula can be found at any well-stocked chemical supply company. The cost of these ingredients in 1976 were: 4 oz. mercuric chloride NF powder: $19.00; 1 lb. magnesium sulfate, purified dried powder: $8.81; 1 lb. potassium iodide USP granular: $5.63; 1 lb. sodium sulfite, anhydrous photo: $1.00.

Unlike many other intensifiers, VMI can be reused and has a long effective working life. I have kept one quart of VMI for over a year. The formula here is for a gallon, but you need mix only enough solution to completely cover the negative to be intensified. The volume decided upon should be measured and dissolved as soon as possible. If the combined dry ingredients are left standing in granular form, the ingredients may begin to separate. The original instructions directed that these chemicals be dissolved in distilled water. I have used both tap water and distilled water. A comparison disclosed no noticeable difference, but if the mineral content of the water in your area is high, use distilled water.

I advise working with one negative or negative strip at a time. Intensifying more than one piece of film at a time creates the danger of uneven intensification and scratching. When intensifying a single frame on roll film, it may be necessary to cut away those frames where intensification creates an undesirable effect.

The intensification process should be done away from bright light. Each time you use the VMI, carefully pour the clear solution into a tray, trying not to stir up the sediment that has settled to the bottom. (A small amount of sediment in the tray won't cause any problems.) A negative is placed emulsion side up in another tray containing water at room temperature and left to soak for ten minutes or until the gelatin has softened. I suggest fixing the film to be intensified in hypo containing a hardener, but when ready for intensification the negative must be free from hypo or stains may occur. After the emulsion has become soft, carefully place the negative, always emulsion side up, in the tray containing VMI. Agitate gently and continuously.

I prefer to use a black rubber or plastic tray when intensifying thin negatives. As the positive areas build in density they begin to reflect light and the dark background of the tray shows the more transparent negative areas as black, permitting a positive image to appear, suggestive of the finished print. Intensification of negatives having greater densities may be done using a white tray, which will allow better observation of the negative image.

The amount of intensification is proportional to the time of treatment and may be followed visually. The color of the negative will change. This is normal for VMI. Thin negatives will appear a bright yellow-orange, while dense negatives will change to a more subtle yellow. This change in color acts as a built-in filter to increase the contrast. One to three minutes of intensification will increase the contrast approximately two to three times. This process may be repeated if a greater degree of contrast is desired. Treatment in excess of ten to fifteen minutes is ineffectual. When the desired degree of intensification is reached, remove the negative from the intensifier and wash for ten minutes in water at 70 F. If sediment has settled on the negative, it may be removed by gently brushing the emulsion with a wet cotton swab. Continue to wash the negative a few minutes longer. Finish by immersing the negative in a wetting agent such as Photo Flo and hang it to dry in a dust free area.

To make a negative that has been intensified with VMI permanent, place it in a one percent solution of sodium sulfide for a few minutes. This is not absolutely necessary, however. I have negatives that were intensified with VMI fifteen years ago and show no signs of deterioration, even though I omitted the sodium sulfide bath.

Local intensification is suggested only for large format negatives, since it is difficult to control the area to be intensified and keep the intensifier from spreading to those areas not intended for intensification. Place the negative in a tray of water (preferably a white tray) after the emulsion has been softened sufficiently (ten to twenty minutes in water 70 F).

When intensifying a large section of the negative, use a large soft-bristle brush or cotton swab to apply the intensifier. Use a small pointed sable watercolor brush (000), the type used for spotting prints, when working with small areas of the negative. The degree of finesse that can be achieved with intensification depends largely upon the size of the applicator and the manual dexterity of the individual using it. The wet negative should be sponged off with a chamois or soft photo sponge before applying intensifier when a definite edge or line is desired. I sometimes blow off the excess water rather than risk scratching the surface of the emulsion. This blowing technique does not allow such sharp edges as with the sponging method.

The portrait of MANELITO (Figure 4) is printed from a thin, flat 35mm negative. Printing this negative on a high contrast paper gave satisfactory separation between highlight and shadow areas, but lost detail in the shadows. VMI corrected this problem, attacking the thin portions of the negative. Intensification also organized the grain pattern to give the illusion of greater image sharpness.

I worked with the negative of THE BIRDS (Figure 5) for many years. This print is the major portion of a highly intensified Tri-X negative. The uncropped negative contains the bottom part of a light bulb. I thought the moonlike shape was the most important part of the image, but finally cut it out when I realized that the shape and texture of the birds were what gave this image its sense of unreality. THE SUBMARINER (Figure 6) was intensified slightly.

Smith-Victor also offered instructions for using VMI as a print intensifier or toner. I found the results inferior when compared with the standard toners and do not recommend VMI for this purpose. Print intensification is basically toning, either by the bleach-and-redevelop method or by the use of a direct toner such as selenium. I have learned that many photographers are now toning their negatives with a selenium toner for archival purposes. I've used selenium toner only to intensify direct positive black and white slides and found it effective where a minimum amount of intensification is needed. VMI is not designed for this purpose because of the discoloration that takes place. Silver intensifiers are recommended where a greater degree of contrast is wanted. They have no effect at all on the color of the positive or negative image. Selenium toners change the tone of the negative or positive image to a slightly warmer color.

There are limitations to the magic of VMI. It cannot increase the amount of detail that was never there in the first place. Intensification may offer an ideal solution to an immediate problem, or you may never consider it worthwhile. If you can afford a little time and effort to experiment with intensification, I think you will find it very rewarding.

FILM	ASA RATING	DEVELOPER	SOLUTION & TIME	AGITATION
Tri-X HP 4	300 to 350	FG-7 D-76 75 to 80 F	FG-7 with sodium sulfite, method 7 D-76 1:1 8¾ minutes	5 seconds in every 30 seconds Complete inversion, then tap bottom against sink

ENLARGER	LENS	LIGHT SOURCE	USUAL APERTURE	USUAL EXPOSURE
Valoy 11 Beseler 4x5	Focotar 50mm *f*/4.5 EL-Nikkor 80mm *f*/5.6 Omegaron 135mm *f*/5.6	No. 212	*f*/8	15 seconds

PAPER	DEVELOPER	SOLUTION & TIME	STOP BATH	FIXER
Kodak Medalist Brovira III Nos. 2 to 6	Dektol Ektaflo	1:2 or full strength 1:9 (Ektaflo) 1½ to 4 minutes	Kodak Indicator 30 seconds	Kodak Rapid Fix 2 baths 3½ minutes in each

WASH	TONING	DRYING	FLATTENING	PRESENTATION
5 minutes running water 2 to 4 minutes hypo eliminator 30 minutes final wash	All types	Air dry on fresh blotters	Print flattener	Drymount on 100% rag Strathmore board Overmatte with same material

Figure 4: MANELITO

Figure 5: THE BIRDS

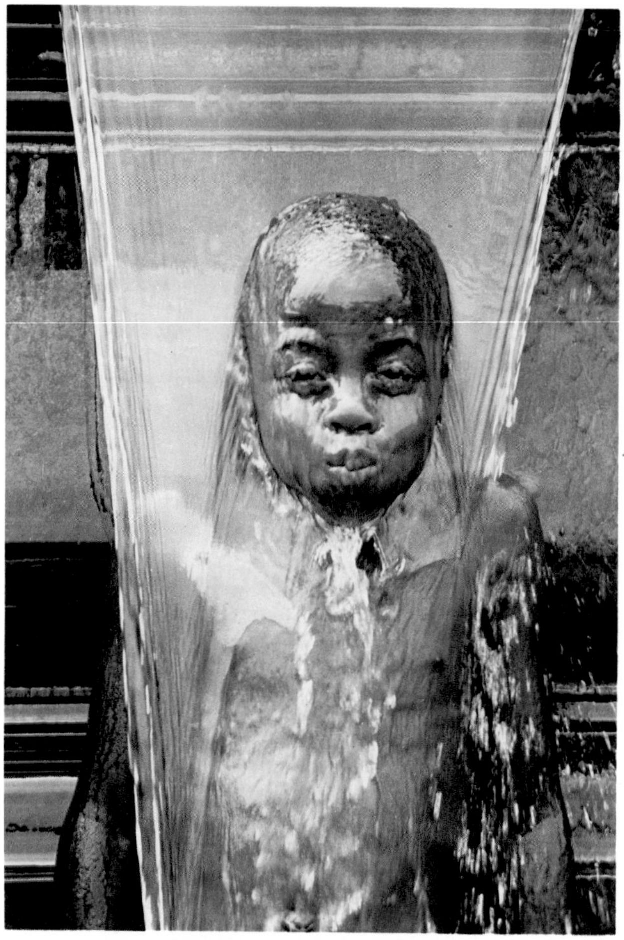

Figure 6: THE SUBMARINER

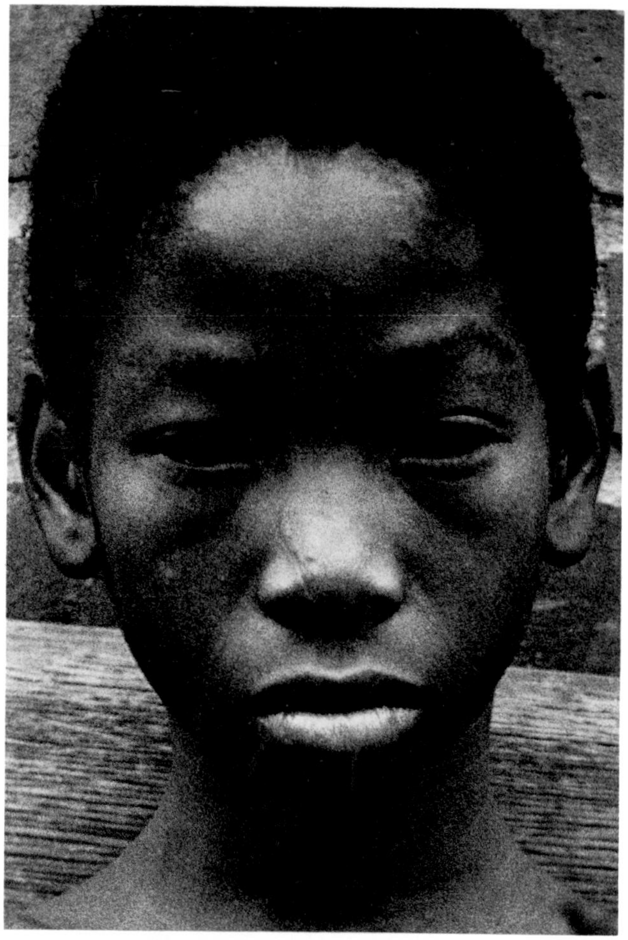

Figure 7: THE SCAR

Figure 8: BLACK BOY

ELAINE MAYES

Elaine Mayes was born in Berkeley, California, in 1938. After receiving a BFA from Stanford University in 1959, she enrolled at the California School of Fine Arts, San Francisco. For the next seven years, Mayes worked as a free-lance commercial photographer.

In 1968 she began teaching at the University of Minnesota. The next year she and Jerry Liebling made a film, THE CLOUDS. In 1971 Mayes illustrated LOVE NEEDS CARE (Little, Brown, Boston, Massachusetts) by David Smith, MD, and John Luce. That same year, she received a National Endowment for the Arts grant and joined the faculty of Hampshire College, in Amherst, Massachusetts.

In 1972 Mayes made FALL, an award-winning short film, and has two films in process. She is Associate Professor of Film and Photography at Hampshire College.

Selected one-woman shows:

1969: Minneapolis Institute of Art, Minneapolis, Minnesota
Massachusetts Institute of Technology, Cambridge, Massachusetts

1970: San Francisco Art Institute

1972: Williams College Art Museum, Williamstown, Massachusetts

1973: Metropolitan Museum of Art, New York
Rhode Island School of Design, Providence
Society for Photographic Education Convention, Albuquerque, New Mexico

1974: Gallery 115, Santa Cruz, California

1975: Rochester Institute of Technology, Rochester, New York

1976: Pratt Institute Photography Gallery, Brooklyn, New York

Selected collections:
Museum of Modern Art, New York
Minneapolis Institute of Arts, Minneapolis, Minnesota
Metropolitan Museum of Art, New York
Philadelphia Museum of Art, Philadelphia, Pennsylvania
Fogg Art Museum, Cambridge, Massachusetts
Boston Museum of Fine Arts

Bill Arnold

I have no definitive technical approach to photography, nor do I consider myself an experimenter. My attitude toward the darkroom is one of searching, much the same as when I photograph. Mostly I have beliefs about the medium, and technique serves to realize the images I find. Photography is part of my life, a way to learn, grow, and feel vital. It is also a difficult and frustrating struggle that tests as well as rewards. I love it passionately and at the same time feel great ambivalence toward it. Since nobody tells me what to do (or how to do it, for that matter), getting started each time, particularly in the darkroom, is a constant battle with inertia and the part of me that wants to do nothing.

I consider myself a "straight" photographer — making camera-produced pictures of situations from the world around me, rendered as full-tonal-range prints. I try not to create or construct photographs but to be open to them. I believe that the photographic process involves seeing, feeling, responding, and I attempt to be subject-oriented since my particular way of looking is unavoidable, a given. By becoming world-focused (a choice), I seem to confront the tension that exists between my interior reality and so-called objective reality. For me, images are to be approached, sought (found), and discovered, and in the photographic process I am given glimpses of things I can't find anywhere else. Whatever I see and photograph is an occurrence or thing revealed.

Normally I do not go out to photograph but take pictures of things that interest me wherever I am. Simple and easily portable equipment is best for this approach, since I walk around wearing my camera most of the time. Any small-roll film camera would suit my style of working, but I prefer using a lightweight 35mm range-finder type. Often on a single roll of film the pictures have been taken under varying conditions (different light intensities), so it is important to simplify the approach to exposure and development and determine an "average standard" in order to make negatives which are always printable.

Experience has shown me that all-around best negatives come from using a fast film (HP4 or Tri-X) fully exposed (when in doubt I overexpose since I prefer to print a dense negative rather than a thin one), developed so that I can obtain a print with detail in the dark areas and a full gray scale. Development is normal or a bit under.

I use fast film for several reasons. It has less contrast than slow film (too much contrast makes pictures too graphic for me), and I usually want as much depth of field and subject sharpness as possible. I prefer to stop down and use a brief shutter speed. Also I like the inherent characteristics of these emulsions and the way the image looks when printed. HP4 seems to need more exposure than Tri-X, so I give it one more stop, even though the manufacturer's rating for both is ASA 400. I don't know the actual ASA I use with either film, since I rarely take a light reading, but simply look at the light and contrast of the situation and expose according to what seems right. For reference I keep a list in my head and consult it when dealing with a specific situation. The following is a very flexible scale I use with Tri-X:

bright sun, landscape with light, open quality, few shadows (image needs good contrast and sharp cloud detail in sky)	f/16	1/250
bright sun with heavy shadows; bright overcast sky; people or objects (when I wish to diminish shadows in midday sun)	f/11	1/250
cloudy bright	f/11	1/125 or 1/250
cloudy darker; city midday, shady side of street in fall or spring; inside house near window on bright sunny day with sun coming through window	f/8	1/125
woods in summer; city winter dark day; further away from window on brighter sunny day	f/5.6	1/125
bright fluorescent interior or shady side of house on sunny day	f/4	1/60
living room at night with bright incandescent illumination; brightly lit commercial area in city at night	f/2	1/60 or 1/30
restaurants, bars, and darker night interiors	f/2	1/8

With HP4, all the above exposures are one stop more, and all these exposures are subject to change, depending on conditions. The main thing is to give ample exposure when shooting. With a flash, I follow the guide numbers recommended by the manufacturer and frequently open up an extra stop just in case.

By far the hardest part of darkroom work for me is getting started in the first place. I have tried all sorts of ploys to make it easier. My current darkroom is at home, and I designed it with the procrastination problem in mind, feeling that it should be a very comfortable, pleasant space. Being in a darkened orange-lit place with the sounds of water and fan (for ventilation is very important) accompanied by acrid odors, are not ideal working conditions for me. Working at home is certainly better than having to go elsewhere, but still I find all kinds of distractions to keep myself away. A friend suggested that I reward myself afterwards, by washing the dishes or cleaning up the house, both tasks that are infinitely easier than taking the first precarious step into the mysterious arena called darkroom.

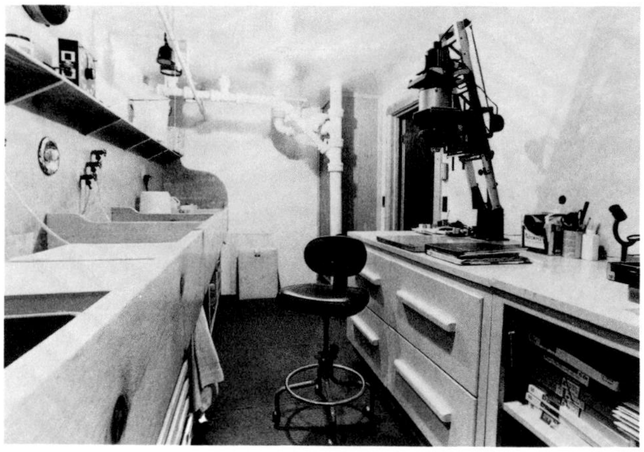

Figure 1.

Figure 2.

Figure 3.

I struggle between compulsive order and the will to abandon all rules, so the kind of darkroom I have, and the way I relate to its procedures, are in keeping with these extremes. The room itself is 7 by 17 feet, with a 2 by 17 foot wooden sink along one side, and the dry counter enlarger area, film drying cabinet, and door along the other side (Figure 1). This arrangement means that I don't have to walk around endlessly. After exposing a print, for example, I just turn 180 degrees to the developer tray. The long sink is extravagant but makes it possible to carry the printing procedure to final washing by sending the print through the chemicals in a continuous motion, although I normally tone the prints with selenium after all the developing and fixing have been completed. With 16 x 20 or larger prints, the long sink is perfect. The most special aspect of the room is the carpeted floor with a thick foam pad underneath, so I can work barefoot for hours without suffering from tired feet. I have a pull-chain light installed above the fixer tray so that I can reach up and turn on the light the instant the print has been sufficiently fixed (one to two minutes, usually).

Another important piece of equipment is the radio-cassette tape machine which provides music while working. Waiting for prints to fix sufficiently or waiting for another thirty seconds during film development are endless repeated times with nothing to do, so I often sing along and sometimes dance to the music.

For developing film, I have made a lengthy search for the definitive developer. Currently I have settled on Rodinal but occasionally use Beseler Ultrafin FD2 or Neofin Red, all very similar in characteristics. In fact, Ultrafin FD2 and Neofin Red are the same chemically, but the packaging is different. Neofin Red is manufactured in Europe and comes sealed in tiny glass vials which insure that each amount is consistently free from oxidation. Ultrafin FD2, which is manufactured in the United States, is packaged in small plastic bottles with screw-top lids, and the packaging doesn't keep the solutions as safely intact. So far I have used it with good results anyway. These developers are more costly than Rodinal and more difficult to obtain, but some people feel they produce negatives with the sharpest grain possible, and sharp grain is a quality I seek. All three developers are considered "high acutance" developers; that is, they produce negatives with very sharp, but not necessarily fine grain. To my knowledge, no developer can do both. For years I used FG 7 (diluted 1:15) or D-76 (diluted 1:1). Both these developers make negatives with rich tones and fine but not sharp grain, so they are suitable for negatives to be printed as small enlargements only. Softness of grain means fuzzy edges on enlargements bigger than 8 x 10 (Figure 2). With Rodinal, Ultrafin FD2, or Neofin Red the grain is very sharp indeed

(Figure 3), and 16 x 20 prints look wonderful.

After the film is in the tank but before developing, I soak it in water (at the same temperature as the developer) for one or two minutes. This soaking procedure prevents air bubbles from lodging on the surface of the film emulsion. If bubbles occur during deveopment, the negatives will have small undeveloped dots which look like dark little disks when printed.

During development I agitate continuously for ten to fifteen seconds during the first thirty seconds, and then agitate (one to three, usually two, tank inversions) every thirty seconds thereafter. Instead of a stop bath I use running water (again at the same temperature as the developer) for thirty seconds, and then I use Kodak Rapid Fix for the time recommended on the bottle. To cut down on washing time and to make sure the fix has been removed, I use a hypo clearing agent before the final wash. Finally, before hanging the film to dry I add two drops of high-concentrate Photo Flo-200 to the tank which is still loaded with film and water.

Ultimately I am not a fine technician, and the technical aspects of photography don't interest me at all. But having a usable and adequate skill is essential, so I seek out methods that best suit the way I photograph and relate to the medium. Simplicity is important because I want to be able to concentrate on the image. If procedure gets too complicated or takes too much time, I get bored and anxious.

For 35mm negatives I use a Leitz enlarger since it is well made and easy to use and holds the negative flat. I prefer to expose for about ten seconds, so I increase the brightness of the bulb with big enlargements (No. 213 for 16 x 20). Occasionally I shoot 2¼, and then I use an Omega D2 with a glass carrier, which keeps the negative flat. I use Componon or Leitz-made enlarging lenses since they are sharp at maximum aperture openings.

When printing, I try to take clues from seeing, from observing how things appear. In most environments nothing is black or absolutely white. "Seeing" and photographing involve light, space, atmosphere, and the ability to discern detail (Figure 4). Most modern photographic papers (which seem to be standardized in relation to graphic principles rather than with what I term revelation of light, space, and object) can only approximate the tonal ranges available in earlier photographic paper emulsions. At best they are not perfect. Good prints come from finding the right paper for individual negatives. I use several different papers—Portriga glossy (III) for subjects that need rich grays and a feeling of depth (Figure 5), Ilfobrom Matte or Portriga Matte (II8) when the image concerns light and a kind of glowing that can float off the paper, and Polycontrast F for 2¼ negatives that need very subtle gradations in the dark and light areas (Figure 6). Poly doesn't work as well with my 35mm format negatives. I use Dektol paper developer 1:2 because it is available everywhere and has a neutral (cold) tone.

While printing I use an acetic acid stop bath. It gives full vent to my desire to abandon proper procedure when measuring. I never measure or dilute the container of 100 percent acetic acid but simply pour the "right amount" into a tray about half filled with water. I use two successive fixing baths, usually Kodak Rapid Fix, for the times recommended on the bottle. Then I use hypo eliminator to cut down on washing time and to insure the removal of fixer from the paper. I use fresh eliminator again after toning.

The color of a Portriga print varies a great deal with developer dilution and development time. Weaker developer and longer development times produce grayer, less brown print tones. And if I wish to turn a No. 3 paper into a No. 2½, I develop the print for thirty seconds in 1:2 Dektol and then use a water bath for another two minutes. Ilford paper doesn't change much after two and a half minutes, but Portriga will continue to develop for five minutes.

I tend to make the prints light and fairly flat, and most dark areas are not printed black but a shade of dark gray, which I deepen by using selenium toner (1:9 or up to 1:12) for three to eight minutes after the fixer has been removed from the paper. The dilution recommended on the bottle is 1:9, but a weaker solution works just as well, although the toning time is longer. With Portriga the print is toned until the greenish-brown image has turned more netural in color, that is, red-brown or purple-brown-black with gray middle tones. With Ilford, I intensify the darks and tone until the black has a barely perceptible purple cast. I decide when the print is sufficiently toned by looking at it.

The height of my compulsive side comes out in my fear of contamination. I am very careful not to get splashes or drops of solution into other solutions: no fixer or acetic acid in the developer, no toner in the fixer or fixer in the toner, no rust—especially near selenium, because it can cause permanent stains. And I am a screaming fanatic about keeping the outsides of storage containers free of dried chemicals, particularly fixer. I have never really tested the effects of contamination, because I loathe making tests. Keeping things neat and tidy and believing contamination to be a problem acts as a focus for order and control.

I use tongs to keep the chemicals and water away from my hands, which dry up and require excessive amounts of hand lotion. I often use Handsafe, "protective barrier against harsh photo liquids," if I get carried away and can't keep my hands out of the solutions. The selenium dye is very toxic, and I've heard it has cumulative poisonous effects on the body, so Handsafe is excellent to use when toning. Surgical gloves are also useful.

The important thing is what the print looks like—is it right for the image. Darkroom technique is a personal matter, and my methods serve the particular aesthetic I search for. I don't feel that one can wrap it up in a week or a year, or five years. It took me about ten years to make what I consider a fine print. It also took me about ten years to comprehend more than a little about my relationship to the medium, and that relationship continues to change.

To me a good print must show everything, must somehow be true to the light, space, form, subject, and content of the picture. It may have no black, or it may have no white. With people and often other subjects, I attempt to make "round" prints. People have qualities of roundness, and portraits should reveal that aspect symbolically. In viewing many of my images, I enter the picture, walk around in it (Figure 7), stand in it or perhaps float. In other pictures, I am more aware of atmosphere (Figure 8) or duration (how long the moment lasts). Some of my pictures are about light and lightness. The print quality must always represent my feeling about the image. I feel that the paper surface itself affects the spatial quality of the photograph, and pictures about light and lightness seem best on matte paper, which makes white areas appear to come forward. This quality means that the light stays on the surface and can possibly "get out" while the blacks recede (Figure 9).

The photographic medium is capable of revealing otherwise hidden aspects of the world. As a mode of visual expression, photography deals with appearances— in what things look like, with relationships, with space, with time (the particular instant), and with metaphor—the way that all the elements of the photograph can be interpreted. I am interested in the camera's "objective eye," in all the images it sees. I am also concerned with the specific qualities of what happens in the picture frame at the moment of exposure, the photograph as evidence of contact between photographer, world, and medium. All these qualities first come alive in the darkroom—the initial look at the developed film, the excitement of seeing an image emerge in the developer tray; then the longest minute of all—waiting for the print to clear in the fixer, so that the light can finally be turned on.

The darkroom is a mysterious, private place where everyday reality makes room for obsession and one's own personal world. Once I'm in there, I lose sight of most everything else. I forget about technique and craftsmanship and, especially with printing, the procedures occur naturally and intuitively. Hours pass unnoticed, even though I'm keeping track of two minutes here, five minutes there. A special freedom happens in the darkroom. It's a place where inspiration, fantasy, and intuition join with technique to produce a vibrant physical expression.

FILM	ASA RATING	DEVELOPER	SOLUTION & TIME	AGITATION
Tri-X HP4	None, uses personal system	Rodinal Ultrafin Neofin Red 68 to 71F	Rodinal: 1:60 14½ minutes Ultrafin: 1:15 10¾ minutes Neofin Red: 1:18 12 minutes	Continuous for first 15 seconds, then 1 to 2 times in every 30 seconds Tank inversion

ENLARGER	LENS	LIGHT SOURCE	USUAL APERTURE	USUAL EXPOSURE
Focomat 1C Omega D2	Leitz Wetzlar 50mm *f*/4.5 Componon 50mm *f*/4 Componon 80mm *f*/5.6	No. 212 No. 213 (16x20)	*f*/8	10 to 20 seconds

PAPER	DEVELOPER	SOLUTION & TIME	STOP BATH	FIXER
Portriga III and II8 Ilfospeed Semi-matte Ilfobrom matte Nos. 2 and 3	Dektol	1:2 2 to 3 minutes	Small amount of 100% glacial acetic acid added directly to water tray 20 to 40 seconds	Kodak Rapid Fix 2 baths 4 minutes in each

WASH	TONING	DRYING	FLATTENING	PRESENTATION
5 minutes running water 2 to 5 minutes hypo eliminator 20 minutes in each of 3 trays, final wash	Selenium 1:9 to 1:12 3 to 8 minutes	Air dry on fiberglass screen	Sandwiched between museum board 10 seconds in drymount press at 200F	Unmounted but overmatted

Figure 4.

Figure 5.

Figure 6.

Figure 7.

Figure 8.

Figure 9.

DUANE MICHALS

Duane Michals was born in McKeesport, Pennsylvania, in 1932. He attended the University of Denver on scholarship and went into the Army in 1952.

Upon his discharge in 1956, he came to New York City and enrolled in the Parsons School of Design. A year later Michals got a job with DANCE magazine as assistant art director and then went to work for Time-Life as a graphic designer. In 1958 he traveled to Russia. The pictures he took on that trip made him decide to become a photographer. He has produced five books—SEQUENCES (Doubleday, New York, 1970), THE JOURNEY OF THE SPIRIT AFTER DEATH (Winterhouse, New York, 1971), THE PHOTOGRAPHIC ILLUSION (Alskog, Los Angeles, 1975) with text by Ron Bailey, TAKE ONE AND SEE MT. FUJIYAMA (Stefan Mihal, New York, 1976), and REAL DREAMS (Addison House, Danbury, New Hampshire, 1976).

Selected one-man shows:

1970: Museum of Modern Art, New York

1972: Delpire Gallery, Paris

1974: Frankfurter Kunstverein, Frankfurt, Germany

1975: Köln Kunstverein, Köln, Germany

1976: Handschein Gallery, Basel, Switzerland
Sidney Janis Gallery, New York

Selected collections:
Bibliothèque Nationale, Paris
Folkwang, Essen, Germany
Stedelijk Museum, Amsterdam, The Netherlands
Boston Museum of Fine Arts

I am concerned with photography and since printing is fundamental to photography, it must be considered, but only as a craft. Printing is to photography what grammar is to literature. When I hear someone brag that they labored for three days in the darkroom to produce a print, my first impulse is to suspect them of being either a terribly incompetent printer or a totally inept photographer. I can't believe that any print is worth three days out of my life. People often make a mystique out of printing to compensate for lack of substance.

I used to go to a gym and the guy who ran it had about five thousand dollars worth of photographic equipment. He would always say, "Listen, what do you think of the Gazebo 17B and their *f*/4.18 lens?" And I'd say, "What the hell are you talking about?" I never knew what he was talking about. But then I would ask, "Well, Lenny, when was the last time you took a picture?" And he'd reply, "Oh, about two months ago." And I'd say, "What was that of?" He'd say he photographed a dog and then he'd bring in these prints of his dog. Somehow something got lost in the shuffle. Values got confused. This is a mistake that schools make also. You go to these schools and these kids all show you gorgeous prints of water running over pebbles. I'd rather see a not so gorgeous mistake of a brilliant idea, an idea that maybe the kid didn't even know how to solve technically. But who cares, because he's talking about something incredible. It's not the medium, it's the message for me.

Once upon a time I was a fanatic too. I would spend a lot of time on printing and get really hung up—do twenty prints of one negative trying to get some little corner right. Then somebody would come in and I'd say, "Now here are twenty prints. Which one . . . can you see what I did?" And they couldn't see a thing. It would be this little blemish over here that had to be smoothed out.

We all have to learn how to print. It's essential to photography. Take lots of pictures. Work in the darkroom. Print a hell of a lot and learn just by making mistakes. It's good to have somebody around who will lean over your shoulder and say, "Listen, you should use a number four filter." But essentially you just have to get into the darkroom and print. Once you learn how to make a gorgeous print, forget it and go on.

I printed for ten years and then about four years ago I stopped. I just couldn't bear it and I had found a printer I liked to work with. There are great advantages and also disadvantages in letting somebody else do the printing. First of all, it's very freeing simply not to have to do it. Also, a printer will often pull something out of a print that you didn't know could be done. My printer has printed a negative completely differently from the way I had visualized it and the print turns out to be just as valid and maybe even better. Sometimes I am astounded by the quality of the print.

But you have to face the fact that nobody can satisfy you as well as you can. Even the best printers can't be one hundred percent. Sometimes they can be terrible. They may produce a print with an area crudely burned in or held back. So it's a little like Russian roulette, but worth it because printing is boring, very boring.

All my printing is done on polycontrast paper with filters, usually a number four. Sometimes a number five paper is used, depending on the negative. I want a good range of grays and always a nice black. However, I don't like prints that are all contrast.

In my work, I try to use the simplest means to achieve the effect I'm after. I use one kind of film, Tri-X, and rate it normally. My taste in light is very specific. I'm like a moth. When I enter a room, I go toward the window. I like a soft, natural light. It's hard to work with but gives a beautiful chiaroscuro effect. Most people are not aware of light as a thing in itself. I go to somebody's house and say, "You have beautiful light." And they say, "Where?" Of all people, photographers should be especially aware of light.

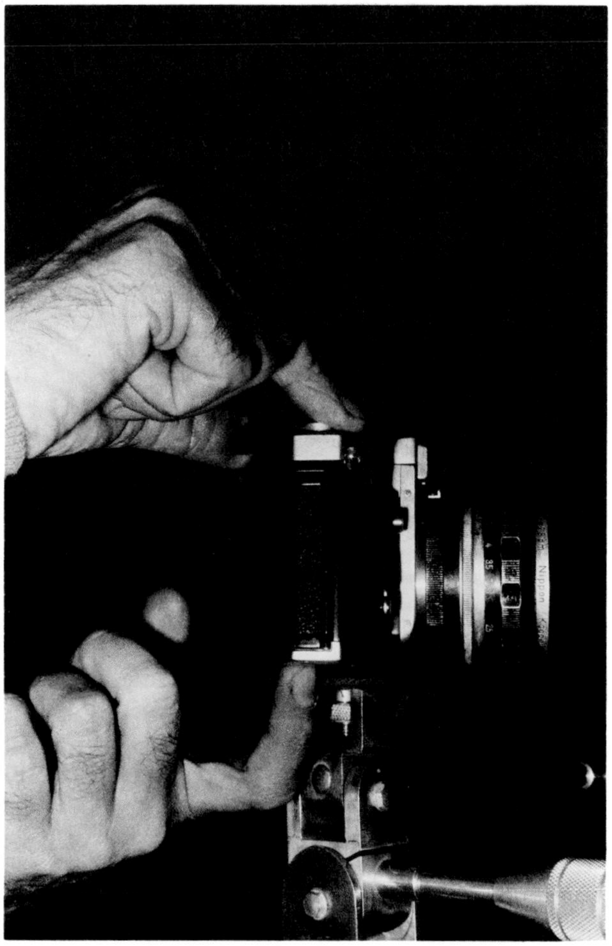

Press rewind and advance simultaneously

Because of the low intensity of window light, I tend to use a tripod, stop down the lens (I always go for depth of field), and do long exposures. I use a Brockway meter which measures reflected light, and I overexpose one stop because I hate thin negatives. I have always felt that if a negative is properly exposed, any idiot can print it. If you have a difficult negative, you're got problems.

A lot of the things I've learned came to me just by using the camera. The more you work and the more you make mistakes, the more you can learn. For instance, when I went to Russia I photographed a bellhop. The film didn't advance and I got a double exposure. I said, "My god, isn't this interesting." I didn't look upon it as a mistake. I felt, gee, the camera can do this.

I did the photograph of THE COUPLE (Figure 4) a long time ago when I first started working with double exposure. It was done with an Argus C3. I feel that this is a successful photograph because I wanted the faces and bodies of the couple to overlap so that when you read her, you don't see him and when you read him, you don't see her. This was hard to control because she was much shorter than he was. First, I photographed him alone. Then I had her stand much closer to the camera. By looking through the camera I could tell when she would appear about the same size as he. He stepped out of the frame and I made the second exposure of her alone. In this way their faces blend perfectly and you get that marvelous thick black edge running between them.

The light source was tungsten bounced off the ceiling. Since you're exposing the same frame twice, you're getting twice as much light on the same negative. Therefore, you should cut each exposure in half. But I expose for double exposures the wrong way. What I do is expose at the total light reading both times. It makes for a much denser negative. Something wonderful happens to the light when you double expose. I think it creates a special quality you don't get any other way.

This is a hard negative to print. Since the man was the first image and received twice the light, he has to be burned in heavily and is slightly fogged. See how much richer the blacks are in the woman's image. The mark on the left of the figures is a tear in the negative. I cried when I saw it. I made four or five negatives and this was the one where the two figures came together best and it was the one the lab tore.

What I love about the picture is the yin-yang effect. That's a beautiful female derriere and that's a beautiful male derriere and that's a beautiul female arm and that's a beautiful male arm. They're marvelous specimens of each sex, making the picture beautiful on that level alone.

The sequence called THE SINISTER DREAM (Figure 5) makes use of negative sandwiches, another way to create double images. Frankly, I prefer to double expose because by doing everything in the camera you don't have to put it all together afterwards. The images are all on one negative and can be printed simply. Also, you get much better quality.

This is a complicated sequence in which a girl has a dream. In it, she sees herself sleeping. A guy comes into the room and puts his hand over her mouth. She suddenly wakes up and we see that the dream was prophetic. The man she dreamed of is actually coming into the room. Pictures two, three, and four are sandwiched negatives.

First, I took the photograph of the girl sleeping in a chair. Notice the picture hanging on the wall. Then I reshot the same photograph but removed the picture to indicate the simplified dream state. I left the chair in the same position so that I would know where the real sleeping girl would appear on the sandwich in two, three, and four. The camera is stationary. In order to keep the girl from overlapping herself in the sandwiched negatives, I had her sit further back against the wall and well to the left of her position in number one. In two, three, and four the man is entering, coming toward her, and putting his hand over her mouth. These images are sandwiches of him making these gestures and the negative of the girl sleeping minus the picture on the wall. The situation was complicated by the fact that I played the intruder and had to keep running back and forth from the camera to the girl. Therefore, I could never tell exactly where I was in the frame. Picture number five shows the girl awakening. I used a blur to suggest shock and movement. The picture is back on the wall, indicating the waking state, and in number six the intruder is moving toward the girl.

Figure 1.

Figure 2.

In printing this sequence, I wanted to emphasize the difference between the dream state and the waking state. Therefore, in two, three, and four, the girl is in darkness and the dream figures are highlighted by crudely holding them back. I wanted them to be surrounded by a balloon of light.

When sandwiching negatives, first clean them thoroughly. Then align the two negatives (Figures 3A and 3B) and place them in the negative carrier. Sometimes it's hard to keep such a thick layer in focus in the enlarger, so it is best to stop down as much as possible, depending on the density of the negatives. The disadvantage here is that if you really stop down, it's going to take a long time to expose the paper.

For me, this sequence is a not so good solution to a very interesting idea. It could have been done better. For instance, the dream figures should not be in the same scale as the waking figures. They should be smaller and up more in the corner. Even the sandwich wasn't quite perfect. You can see the negative borders come into the frame in two, three, and four. But I don't mind. I love the way the figure of the intruder emerges from the darkness in number two.

Let's go back to picture number five of the sequence for a moment to talk about the use of blurs. This is another technique I discovered just by working. My first blur was a mistake, and then I realized how useful it could be to communicate movement and certain states of mind. To make a blur, I stop down the lens as far as possible and use a slow shutter speed. A second is just long enough to get a nice blur. Then I run the person through the gesture at varying speeds. I tell them to think about doing it in slow motion. You can't control a blur. If people move too fast, they blur too much (Figure 1). But if you get the right amount of movement, the blur gives you just enough information (Figure 2).

Here's a portrait I did of Harry Wilkes in bits and pieces (Figure 6). I thought it would be interesting to do a composite portrait of a person, showing different parts of his anatomy, parts that you would never really see, like the belly button or the left ear. Photographing one person, I did the perspiration on his forehead. When you look at a person, you receive many impressions about him. You don't really see him physically except maybe his face. There are marvelous parts of the body to explore, the joining of neck and shoulder or where the hips fit into the torso. These are very beautiful. This portrait is treated the same way as the rest of my work: Nikon F, Tri-X, daylight. Here sunlight was very strong, so I hand held the camera and got good depth of field.

This is another way to investigate the portrait, not just a rendering of somebody sitting there looking interesting. All I'm doing is expanding the possibilities and it fits in with my idea of seeing things sequentially (Figure 7).

Figure 3A

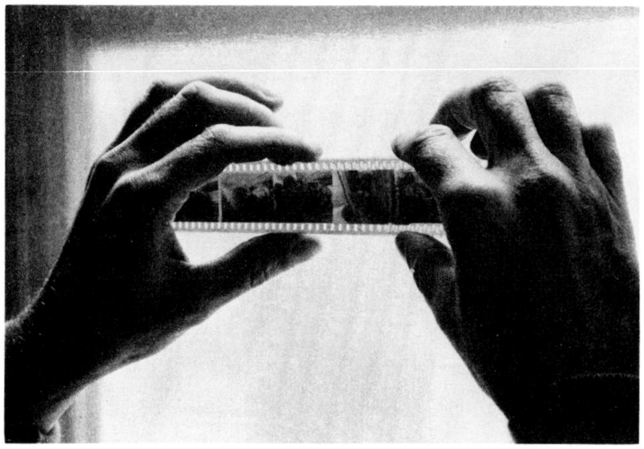

Figure 3B

FILM	ASA RATING	DEVELOPER	SOLUTION & TIME	AGITATION
Tri-X	400	FG-7 ——— 68 F	1:10 ——— 7 minutes	5 seconds in every minute ——— Tank inversion with slight twist after return to upright position

ENLARGER	LENS	LIGHT SOURCE	USUAL APERTURE	USUAL EXPOSURE
Omega D2	EL-Nikkor 50mm *f*/2.8	No. 213	*f*/8	6 to 8 seconds

PAPER	DEVELOPER	SOLUTION & TIME	STOP BATH	FIXER
Polycontrast F	Dektol	1:2 ——— 1½ to 2 minutes	28% glacial acetic acid solution ——— 1½ minutes	Kodak fixer ——— 2 baths ——— 5 minutes in in each

WASH	TONING	DRYING	FLATTENING	PRESENTATION
5 minutes running water ——— 5 minutes Perma Wash ——— 15 minutes final wash	None	Air dry on fiberglass screen	Sandwiched between museum board in drymount press	Under glass

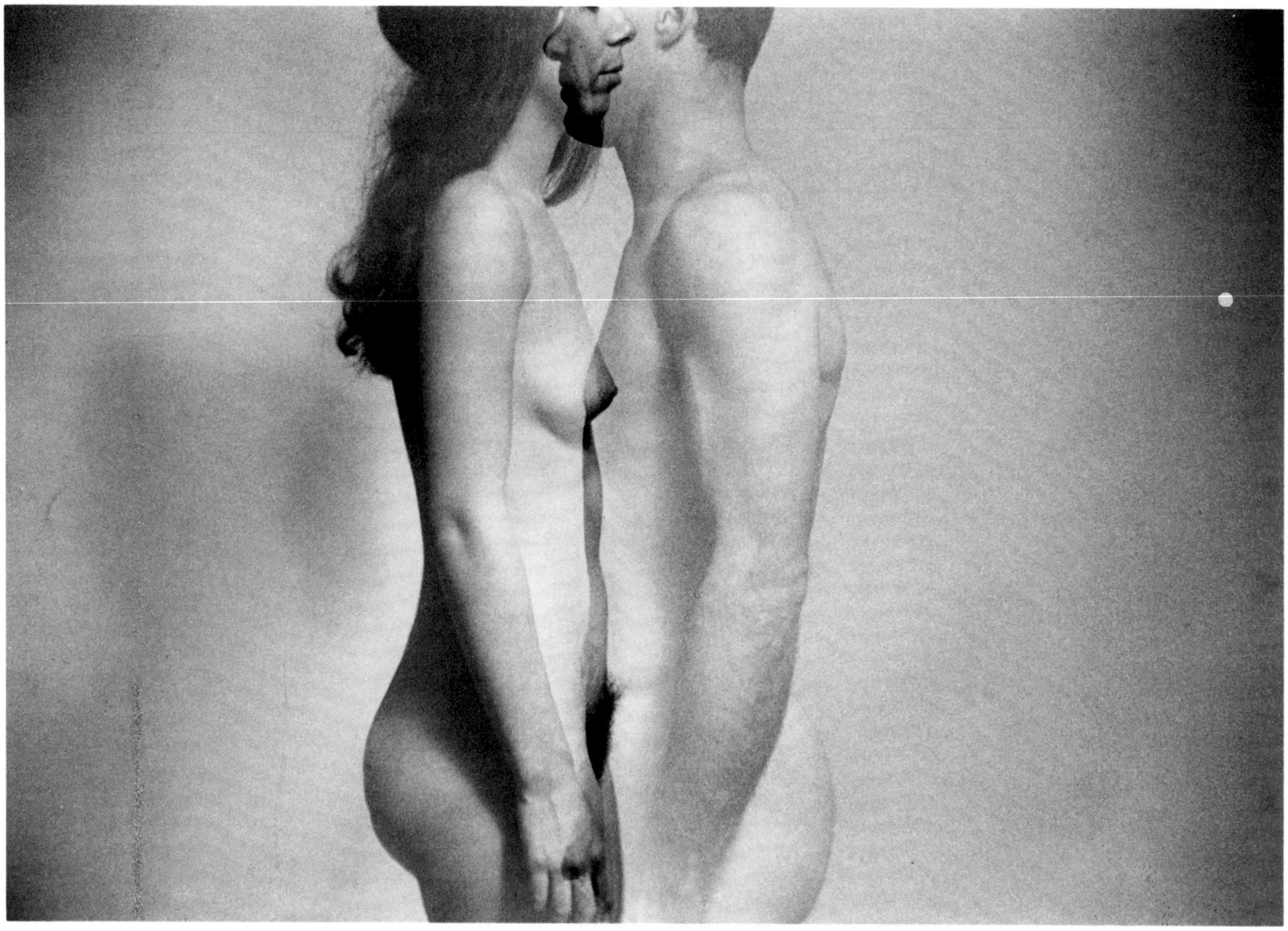

Figure 4: THE COUPLE

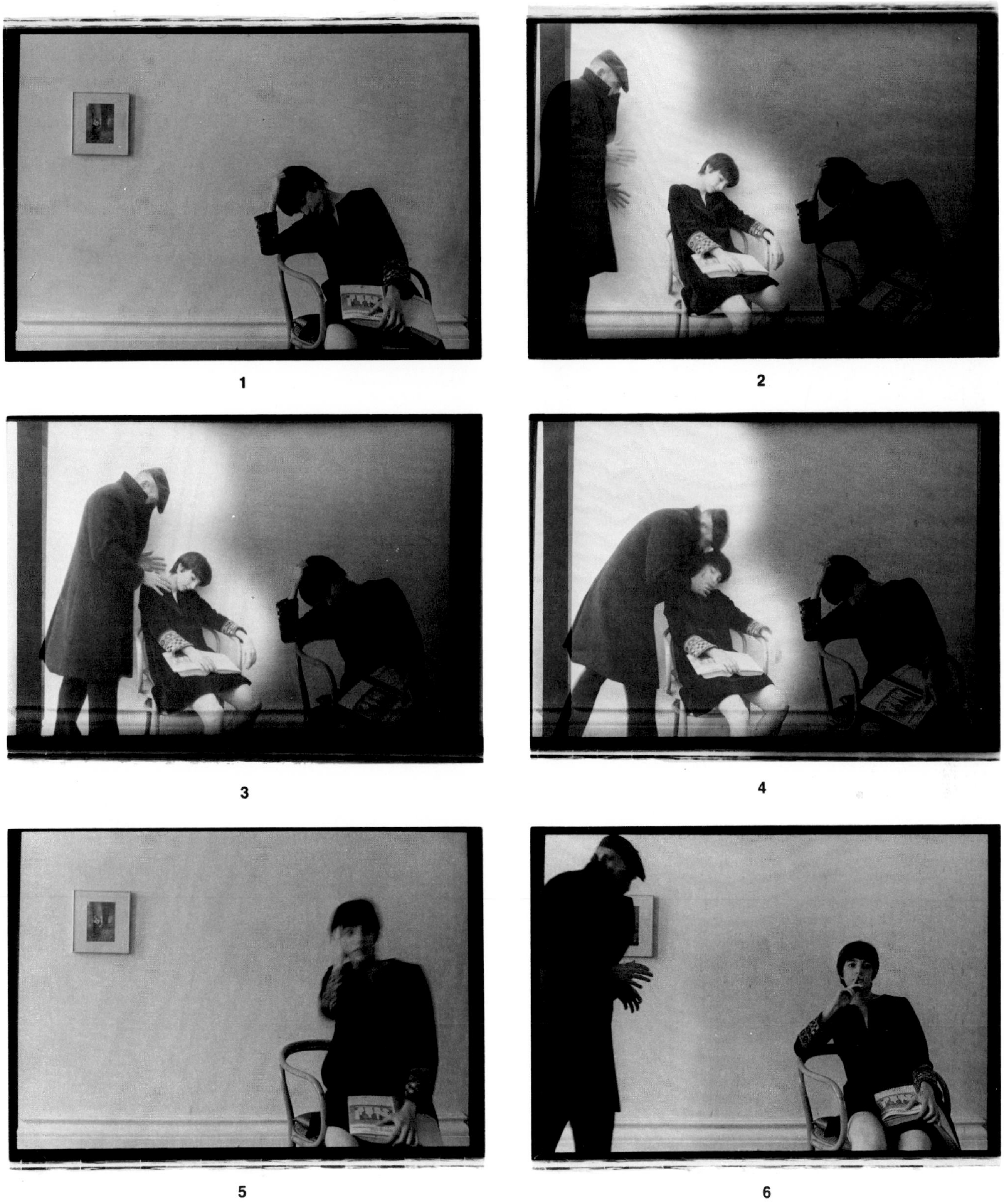

Figure 5: THE SINISTER DREAM

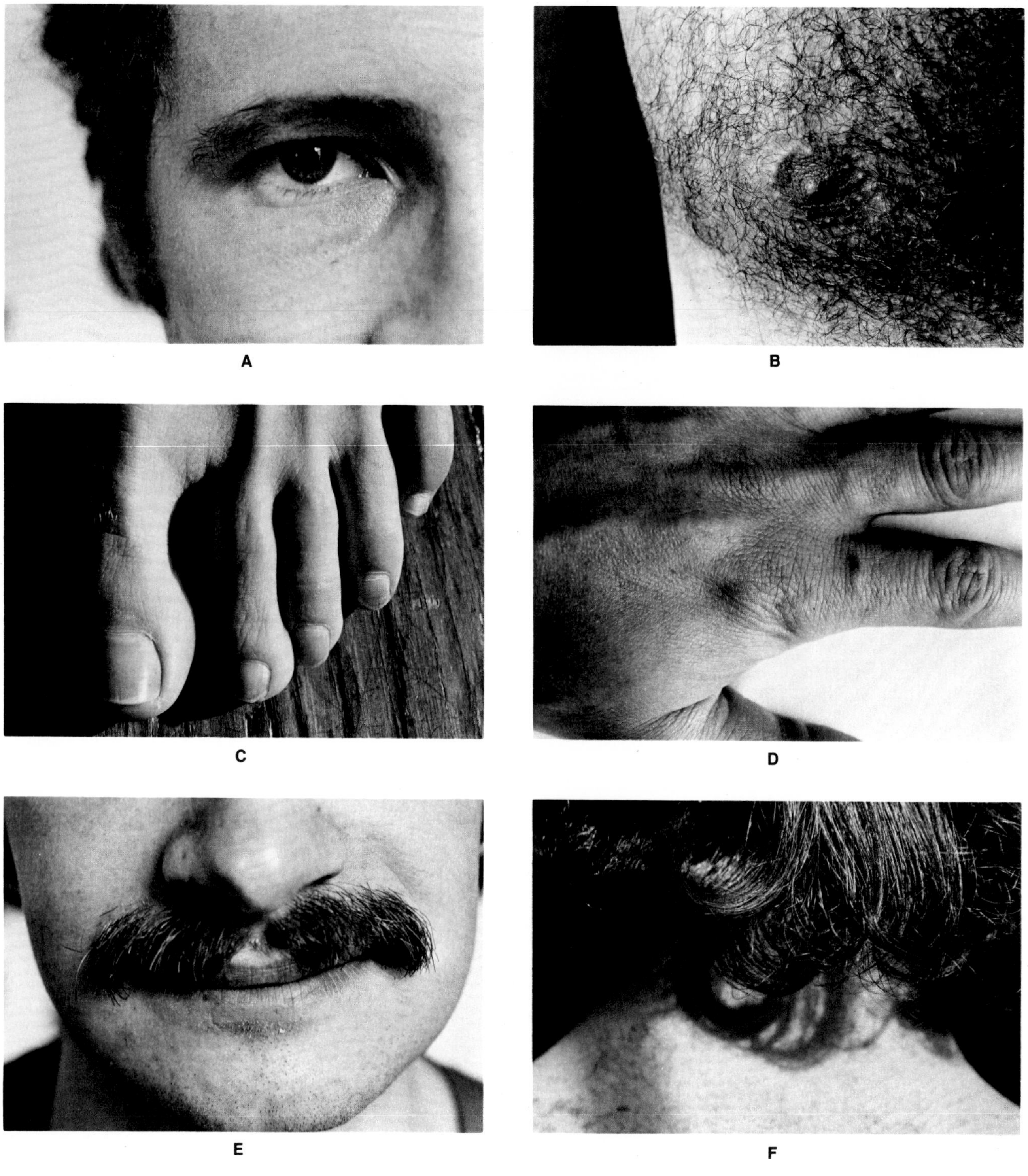

Figure 6: PORTRAIT OF HARRY WILKES

Figure 7: ANDY WARHOL 1973

W. EUGENE SMITH

W. Eugene Smith was born in Wichita, Kansas, in 1918. He first used photography as an aid in school assignments and during the last two years of high school, free-lanced for local newspapers.

In 1936 he entered the University of Notre Dame but soon left for New York City to join the NEWSWEEK staff.

In 1938 he joined the Black Star Agency and his work began to appear in national magazines. He signed a contract with LIFE magazine in 1939, and in 1941 resigned and began to free-lance.

In 1943 Smith became a war correspondent. He then joined the Ziff-Davis Publishing Company staff and went to the Pacific. Leaving Ziff-Davis, he rejoined LIFE in 1944 and continued to cover the fighting in the Pacific. In May 1945, Smith was critically injured.

In 1947, after two years of medical treatment, Smith returned to full-time work for LIFE, where he produced major photo essays such as "Trial by Jury" (1948), "Hard Times on Broadway" (1949), "Spanish Village" (1951), "Nurse Midwife" (1951), "Chaplin at Work" (1952), "My Daughter Juanita" (1953) and "A Man of Mercy" (1954). He was awarded a Guggenheim Fellowship in 1956 and another in 1957 to work on a photo essay on Pittsburgh.

In 1958 he taught a course at the New School for Social Research in New York, "Photography Made Difficult."

Smith went to Japan in 1961 to work for Hitachi Limited, and in 1964 his Hitachi-sponsored book, A CHAPTER OF IMAGE, was published. That year he was appointed to the President's Committee on Photography.

In 1969 he received a third Guggenheim Fellowship and also a National Endowment for the Arts grant for the publication of his monograph W. EUGENE SMITH (Aperture, Millerton, New York).

In 1971 Smith returned to Japan with his wife Aileen. They received a National Endowment for the Arts grant to finish work on the book MINAMATA (Holt, Rinehart, and Winston, New York) which was published in 1975 in conjunction with a show at the International Center for Photography in New York City.

Selected one-man shows:

1941: Museum of Modern Art, New York
1969: Rochester Institute of Technology, Rochester, New York
1970: George Eastman House, Rochester, New York
1971: Jewish Museum, New York
1974: City Auditorium, Minamata, Japan
1975: International Center for Photography, New York
1976: The Witkin Gallery, New York
1977: State University, Wichita, Kansas

Selected collections:
George Eastman House, Rochester, New York
Museum of Modern Art, New York
Art Institute of Chicago

Dick Swift

When I go out to shoot, I never change lenses on my camera. I change the camera, and if I'm working at full strength, I usually carry two sets of them, different makes for black and white and color film, so that I know by the very feel of the camera which film I'm using.

I work with five cameras and drape them three down the front and two on my shoulder. The lenses I carry have shifted a bit as the ultra-wide-angle ones improved. When I did "Country Doctor" (1948), the fastest available wide angle lens was the 35mm *f*/4 Biogon, and it was a wonderful lens. So I use the 35mm and the 85mm as my two basic lenses. The only lens I leave out is the normal 50mm or 55mm unless I need an extremely high-speed lens. When I did "Nurse Midwife" (1951), the rooms were so small I couldn't relate the midwife and patient in the same picture with a 35mm so I bought a 28mm. It was *f*/8, and with those dark rooms it presented one hell of a problem. (I used a small strobe.)

In a delicate story such as "Nurse Midwife," you'd think you'd have to be very discreet. You just don't want to move in on some backwoods person, clanking equipment. But I found that the shock of seeing me walking around with five cameras on me was no worse than if I just carried one.

I try to overcome the noise of the shutter and equipment by sheer acceptance. Where people are nervous about a camera, I go through a roll of film as fast as I can. If they're trying to pose for me, I try to catch them off guard, to the point where they give up on all that, get bored, and go about what they were doing. Then I can get close to someone, and even with a loud shutter they won't be aware of me.

In spite of all the cameras and loud shutters, I try to move with great quiet and never project myself into the room if I can possibly help it. I prefer to stay back in such a way that I'm not noticed. I think my shyness is one reason why I have become so intimate with my subjects. If they accept me, I'm not pushing a camera into their faces.

For the "Nurse Midwife" story I was using mostly Leicas, but now I use single-lens reflexes—Minoltas, Pentaxes, Nikons. Although I'm still fond of the range finder camera, I do love that ability to edge in for an extra fraction of an inch and have something absolutely lined up. I think the single lens reflex gives you the best control.

If the light is difficult, I sometimes take a meter reading, but then all I do is give the longest exposure possible under the circumstances, and develop the film by inspection.

Once in the darkroom, to cut down on time I'll often develop two rolls of film on each reel. This turns a four reel tank into an eight reeler. I open up two film cans, cut the film off the spools, and put the two tails together so that they curl away from each other (Figure 1A). This tells me the films are back to back, emulsion side out. Then I curve the pair

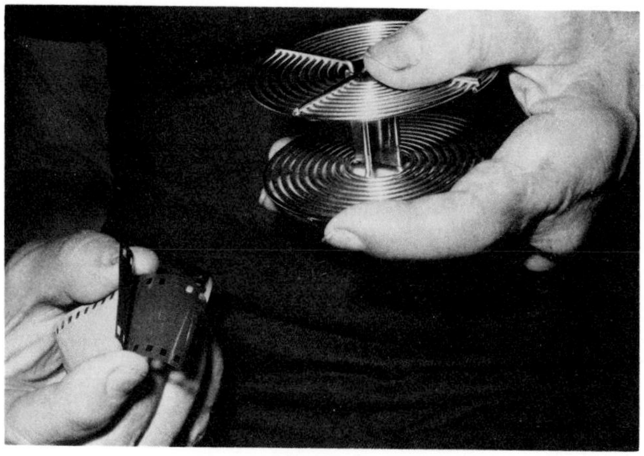

Figure 1A

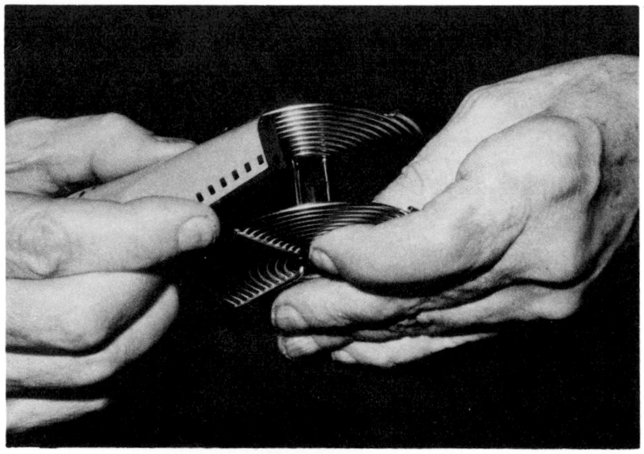

Figure 1B

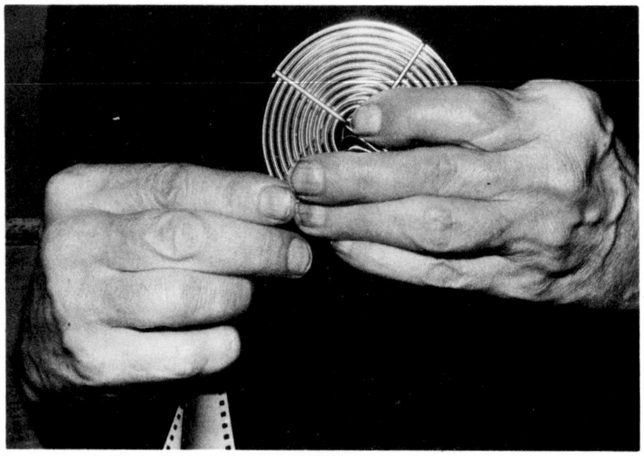

Figure 1C

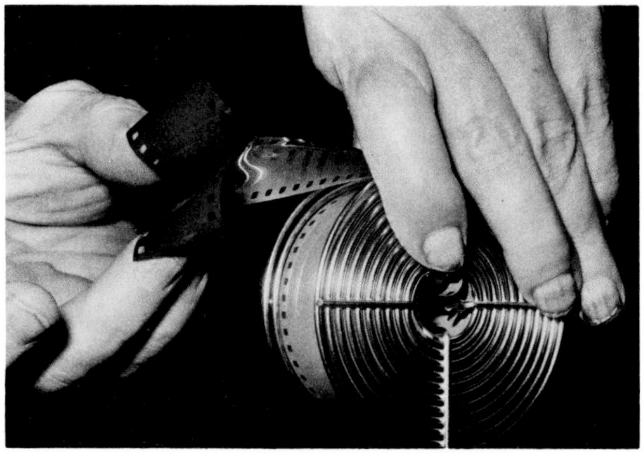

Figure 1D

slightly with the thumb and forefinger of my right hand, and insert them into whatever kind of reel I happen to be using (Figure 1B). As I thread the film I try not to drag tightly on it (Figure 1C). I always run into trouble at the end because there are a couple of inches of film that just don't fit on (Figure 1D). I've discovered that by shooting four blanks at the head of a roll I can cut off more film from the tongue. Actually, I try to leave two or three frames unexposed at the end of the roll, too, just so there won't be any accidents when it is dried. I'm happy with a thirty exposure roll, but sometimes in an intense situation I keep right on going. I've been known to tear the end of the film off the spool.

To process film, I used to use D-76 with ten times the normal amount of borax of Kodalk and run the film up to ten minutes—twelve, if I really had to push it. I would never use raw D-76, but always added a little of the old, just to take the edge off the grain.

With the Minamata pictures I went back to plain D-76 (two parts developer to one water) and developed from twelve to twelve and a half minutes. Sometimes I'd get up to thirteen and a half minutes. This has no relation to Eastman's instructions. The kind of negative I get is full of guts in the shadows, so that I can always print them down if I want. I'm of that old school which exposes for the shadows.

In the early days it was easy to develop by inspection. You had these blind films you could hold up to a bright safelight and just look through. Now you turn on the dim green safelight a couple of minutes beforehand so your eyes get used to the light. Then, at eight minutes or so, you take the film out of the developer, hold it a foot and a half or so from the light, and turn it until the light reflects off the surface of the film for just a few seconds. It's a question of being able to evaluate the blacks and grays. Usually a certain tone of charcoal comes out being satisfactory to me. A black man standing against a black background is a more difficult inspection problem than if he were standing against a white wall. I always try to mark rolls as to what kind of light they were exposed under, and as to general subject. Then I try to develop film in groups so that I can anticipate the problems I have to face.

But I'm not as good at it as Bernie Hoffman was. He used to have a pair of scissors, and as he was going through a roll of negatives, he would start clipping it up and developing this section more and that section less. I don't carry it that far, but inspection certainly comes in handy.

In the Minamata story I think there were only two rolls that were developed by inspection, simply because the situation was so difficult. It's interesting to know that in winter we used to start with developer at 76 F and come out at about 67 F. Then we'd put the film in hypo at around 69 F, and it would get down toward 60 F. Then we'd wash it in 35 F water. Afterwards, the negatives were sometimes heat dried. My landlord would build a wood fire for the baths in the same dirty kitchen we used for developing, and the sparks would start flying with my wet negatives hanging there . . . it gave me the dirtiest negatives I ever had to spot in my life.

As long as a negative is printable, it's all right with me. The impossible light conditions I've worked under have made me struggle. Sometimes I mumble to myself, but then I say, "Oh hell, I'll just print it." You don't always have to fight the light. Sometimes you can use it to make an entirely different kind of photograph. But if it's a photograph I've really had to fight for and the content is there, I'll print it somehow. This is something only I can control in the darkroom.

There's nothing in photography I hate worse than the discipline of the darkroom (Figure 2), and yet I have spent all these years printing. The reason is very simple. I want the damn pictures to say what I want them to say. I want to subdue those things that are not important to the statement, and I want to make sure that the important things are open, clear, and direct. Making my own print is the only way to fulfill what I saw when I made the photograph.

People think I make dark prints, but a good Smith print is not dark. You get a feeling of darkness, but you will see that all the important detail is very accessible. The secondary detail is quieter in tone. There is no way in the world you can tell anybody else to do this. I've had a couple of very good printers try to print for me, and sometimes I could accept their prints, but these didn't have the subtleties, the kind of statement I wanted to make.

My printing style has evolved out of my work for publications. In an effort to balance prints and make them work for engraving, I evolved a style that I happen to like for my own work. The two approaches coincide, except that I give the printer the worst print. It's usually a little lighter, although you can't totally outguess a printer. I have illustrations from several sources made from the same print, and the differences between them are fantastic.

Yesterday somebody shocked me by bringing over sixteen prints I had made at the time of "Spanish Village" (1951). They were absolutely beautiful. Whether the paper has changed or I can't print as well, I don't know, but there was an openness I just can't get with the present papers. I'm not happy with any that I'm printing on. I have to work harder to get the openness I want, or I should say I have to work harder with ferricyanide. I don't feel that bleaching is dishonest to the reality of the image, because it helps me state clearly what I feel the true reality to be.

Basically, I bleach to bring back what is not held strongly in the film or the paper. The better these are, the less I have

Figure 2.

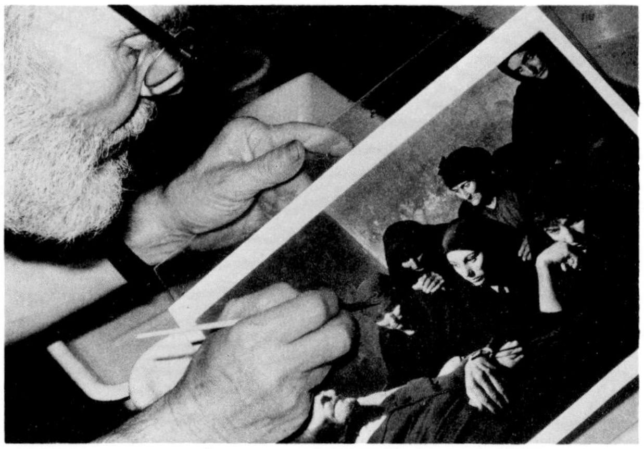

Figure 3.

Figure 4: Printing tools

to bleach. I can emphasize skin tones with ferricyanide. For instance, just a touch along certain highlight areas on the face or arms will give an almost three-dimensional feeling. It can also produce a much greater sense of texture. I like a surface that doesn't appear to have a piece of cellophane between it and the viewer. I want a piece of cloth to feel like cloth when you look at it. Bleach can be used to remove that sheet of gray that comes over printing papers sometimes.

I fill the little cup in the palm of my hand with ferricyanide, and mix it with ¼ cup of water. (If I'm in a hurry I add more ferricyanide.) I wipe the hypo off the print with my hand (you can blow it off also.) Then I paint the ferricyanide on with an 000 sable brush, or a cotton ball, or Q-Tip (Figure 3). Oftentimes, I leave large areas of the print covered with hypo, flood it with ferricyanide, and set it back down in the hypo, quick. You always have to get the print back into the hypo, fast, before the bleaching has truly set in. Afterwards, I like to put the print through a second, fresh hypo bath.

The atmosphere of the darkroom is important. It has to be very open, very comfortable, so that you have room to move around in while working. And it must have music. I don't think I could ever stay in the darkroom without it. It has been my best concert place. It's also where I meditate. I do a lot of things in the darkroom all at once.

Positioning of equipment is important. When I'm trying to print rapidly, it speeds things up if I can glance at the print I just made to get an idea about what to do with the next one.

I have an automatic foot timer that gives me great control. Most timers are fixed so that you push a button and the enlarger light goes on. But to my mind, it is too hard to get your hands into position from the time you flick the switch. Many times a certain area will take as many as fifteen exposures for burning in. I have the timer fixed so that it is controlled by a foot switch, and I have to keep my foot on the switch if I want to give the set exposure. In other words, I give the exposure with the foot switch and the timer gives me the time. When it comes to those fractions of a second, a bit of light here, a little shading there, my foot switch overrides the timer, and the enlarger light stays on as long as I keep my foot down. It could be half a second or five seconds. When it goes on, the foot switch also turns off the safelight over the enlarger. I find it is one of the most important devices in printing. I also have a long string across the darkroom. I can grab it anywhere to turn the overhead light on.

The enlarger I use is an old, discontinued Leitz Valoy, with a single condenser and a light diffuser lid. This is the best balance of light that I have ever used. The lens that's on the enlarger right now is a Minolta made for printing color. When made for color, it is well corrected, so that you get sharp grain all the way across the print. I have something like twenty enlarger lenses, and once a year I put a focusing grid into the enlarger and make a very systematic set of tests. I've never quite figured out which is the best lens.

Many people think that one criterion of a good print is brilliantly sharp grain from corner to corner, but I don't give a damn about all that brilliance of grain. If I'm doing a portrait, I would much rather have that grain broken up a little so there's more modeling in the face. I find that with the double condenser all that sharpness is so intense it breaks up the sharpness of the image. You have such a pattern of grain across the face that you don't get the modeling you want. That's why I go for a single condenser and slight diffusion.

To get the diffusion, I use a piece of black wire screen (Figure 4) held near the lens. My nervous shake makes sure it doesn't give a screen pattern. I can often expose a print up to 100 percent with the screen and not destroy enough of the sharpness to bother me, while getting better modeling, a better feeling of the texture. However, I usually don't use it more than 25 or 50 percent, just to break up the grain a bit.

If I want just a little more diffusion, I use a piece of black stocking, but only for a short time. If you use the stocking through much of the exposure, you get an odd kind of fogging. Sometimes I actually use a diffusion filter. Say a print has an ugly, uneven sky: a diffusion filter helps smooth it out, especially if the development has been bad. One must decide whether or not the picture is too diffused. These things must be used sparingly. When I smoked, I blew smoke under the lens. (I also used to drop ashes in my developer. Some people thought it was my secret formula.)

Most of the time I use selenium toner to intensify and slightly solidify grayish tones. I mix the selenium one to ten parts water and tone for eight to twelve seconds. Sometimes in night scenes I may go up to thirty-five or fifty seconds. This gives just an edge of toning, so you can't be sure if the print's been toned at all. I've noticed I have to overdo this a little bit, because if I dry a print on a heat drier most of the toning disappears. Also, I understand that selenium is supposed to make the print last a little longer. My prints usually get scratched as soon as I send them out, so I don't know why I worry about them lasting, but it should make those people who buy my prints happy.

Sometimes, when I have an extremely difficult negative to print, one made under impossible light conditions, a copy negative can make a difference; but it can also be very difficult to print from. It's not just a simple copy that comes out like the original print. Unless it's a contact print, the values change, and I have to ferricyanide again to open up shadow detail that has disappeared with the increased contrast. There is a tendency for the negative to be a little sharp in the middle tones. It's sometimes as hard to print as the original negative, but a copy negative helps.

To make one, I used to use the old Polaroid film that was based on Panatomic-X. It was a little contrasty, but the copies I made with it came out almost better than any special copy film I ever used. THE WALK TO PARADISE GARDEN (Figure 5) is printed from a Polaroid copy negative. Figure 5 is a straight print from it. Someone lost the original negative, which was difficult to print because some of the leaves were overexposed and some were too dark. I was trying to keep most of the leaves around the path light but with detail.

The negatives the Compo Lab in New York made for me on gravure film were quite nice also. Compo was very cooperative in trying to make these things work, but I was always overexposing compared with other people. I always feel I can burn down. At its best, the copy negative is almost like your original print, and it does diminish some of the terrible problems in a difficult negative. I don't mind signing my name to a copy negative print if I've made it and it's good. After all, I'm trying to extract from any negative a photograph that expresses what I want to say. I don't think one more mechanical process takes anything away.

THE DEATH SCENE (Figure 6) from "Spanish Village" (1951) was an impossible negative. There was one light over the dead man's head, and the person seven or eight feet away was wearing a black gown. Try to bring everything together from that head to the black gown. It's just impossible. I wanted to shade off to the right with the person in the upper right being darker than any of the other figures, but I wanted to shade off very gently and hold some detail.

The longest time it has ever taken me to make a print was five days and five nights. That was the lead picture in the Schweitzer story (Figure 7). The problem again was bad equipment. I was using an 85mm lens that was not properly baffled against an overbright backlight. It's a beautiful lens for sharpness, modeling, and things like that, as long as the light is behind you. But with the backlight, a sheet of fog came down over the entire bottom of the picture. Any commercial printing outfit would have simply thrown this negative out, but I wanted it for the lead picture, and I went nuts trying to print it. I had to burn down darkly every bit of detail in that photograph to get shadows under the hat, detail in the face, etc., etc. Then after I got it much too dark, I had to bring everything up, detail by detail, leaf by leaf, arm by arm. One area alone would take five hours to ferricyanide, and then five hours and one second later I made one jab too many, and wham, I'd have to start all over again! I can assure you that I'm never going to print the original again. This print is from a copy negative, and I think it works out fairly well. The copy negative is a little harsher than the original. I have to open up the highlights on the cheeks a bit more. It requires softening, but I can probably get a print from this negative in an hour instead of five days and five nights.

All those legends about my taking a week to make a print are based on this experience. But I also remember once when I got home from an assignment and found I only had twelve sheets of paper and eight negatives to print. I made them on the twelve sheets.

As far as fast printing is concerned, I think I can print just about as fast as anybody in the world. I once made eight hundred 5 x 7 proof prints in one day, operating two enlargers, one with each foot. (Somebody else developed for me.) But those were proofs and that was my compromise with LIFE. I never showed the editors contact sheets. I'd make a fairly generous selection of 5 x 7's for them to look through, and we'd start arguing from there.

The negative for the photograph of SCHWEITZER AT HIS DESK (Figure 8) wasn't a bad one. The exposure itself was 1/5 or 1/2 second, along with a strobe that I covered with a handkerchief and bounced off the dirty brown floor. If I had just used the oil lamp, there would have been a sharp shadow across one side of Schweitzer's face and none of this softness of detail in the background. The long exposure gives the feeling of the lamplight, and the strobe gives the detail. When it came to printing, I had to bring down the whites around the edges on the left where some papers were intruding. They would have cut in like little ragged edges. And I had to burn in the whole shade to get it down so you could see the flame against it. Then I ferricyanided the flame. It took almost three hours to get the first good print.

The photograph of TOMOKO IN THE BATH (Figure 9) from the Minamata story represents another one of those impossible lighting situations. There were high windows almost the length of the picture. If I had used only the light that was entering the room, I would have had no shadow detail on the near side of the mother's body at all. In this photograph I also happened to use a small, battery-operated strobe, this time bounced off a fairly clean brown ceiling instead of a dirty brown floor.

There is a basic exposure for the whole picture, in which I dodge the area of the mother's right breast. This is all the dodging necessary, except for the water at the edge of the tub. I burn in various sections of the white towel around the mother's head, something like sixteen times the original exposure, giving the face just one extra shot. Then I burn in the face of the child, maybe six, eight times the original exposure. In other words, the child's face takes much more exposure than the face of the mother or the main body of the picture. And I give the iron edges of the tub a very narrow exposure. I burn in both ends of the picture to make sure there is no grayness creeping up from the edges—it must get darker toward the sides. I burn in the stomach and chest of the child just once or twice. In the upper-left-hand part, you see some boards, or lines, going along. This is where the edge of the bathtub meets the back wall. I give three or four exposures just to that area, and then I give the whole bottom part (masking off all the body sections except a touch of the child's left foot) maybe another four or five exposures, so this would get progressively darker. Then I burn in the top highlight on her right leg as steadily as I can, but it's very awkward (Figure 10). I use either a formation of my fingers or a cardboard cutout. Mostly I use my hands, even the fingers that are misshapen.

I burn in the left leg to some extent, but I never burn in the top area long enough because it's so strenuous that at this point I'm too tired. I use a 250-watt bulb in the enlarger with a heat-absorbing glass negative carrier. It holds the negative flat, which keeps it from buckling when the basic exposures are short and the burning in long.

If the small prints seem difficult, those four and a half foot prints we made for the Minamata show at the International Center for Photography were really murder. We had a couple of 2 x 4's that went across floor beams and put a piece of plywood on them so we could move without shaking the print. We took the enlarger off the stand and turned it around so it would project down. The burning in was the same as for small prints, but the basic exposure was much longer. It probably took at least fifteen or twenty minutes of exposure for each sheet of paper. And then, of course, we had a very narrow span in which to develop and get the print into the hypo. We put narrow boxes together, lined them with plywood, and had two rollers of plastic piping. We would ram the paper onto the rollers and into the developer, and roll it as quickly as we could from one roller to the other. I suppose the tray wasn't more than a foot and one half by two feet, and the paper was about four feet wide. When I ferricyanided, we put a big tray outside. It took so many gallons of hypo to fill that tank it was unbelievable. And since we did a lot of this in winter, I had kerosene heaters to warm my front, but I was freezing from the rear. It was kind of messy.

As I said before, I absolutely despise printing. I look at the negative, and I look at the print. I come face to face with all the mistakes I made. In the darkroom it is my problem to overcome the mistakes. I know the print I want, and know I'll probably get it, but it's sheer drudgery. My formula for successful printing remains ordinary chemicals, an ordinary enlarger, music, a bottle of Scotch, and stubbornness.

FILM	ASA RATING	DEVELOPER	SOLUTION & TIME	AGITATION
Tri-X	400	D-76 ——— 68 F	2:1 (D-76 — 2 parts water — 1 part) ——— 12 to 13½ minutes	15 to 20 seconds for 1 or 2 turns ——— Flat bottom

ENLARGER	LENS	LIGHT SOURCE	USUAL APERTURE	USUAL EXPOSURE
Valoy 11	Minolta C.E. Rokkor-X 50mm F/2.8	No. 213	*f*/8	Varies

PAPER	DEVELOPER	SOLUTION & TIME	STOP BATH	FIXER
Polycontrast F	Dektol	Full strength ——— 1:1	Water	Kodak F-6 ——— 2 baths ——— 5 minutes in each

WASH	TONING	DRYING	FLATTENING	PRESENTATION
5 minutes running water ——— 5 minutes Perma- Wash ——— 15 minutes final wash	Selenium ——— 1:10 ——— 8 to 50 seconds	Air dry on fiberglass screen	None	Drymount on 100% rag board

Figure 5: THE WALK TO PARADISE GARDEN

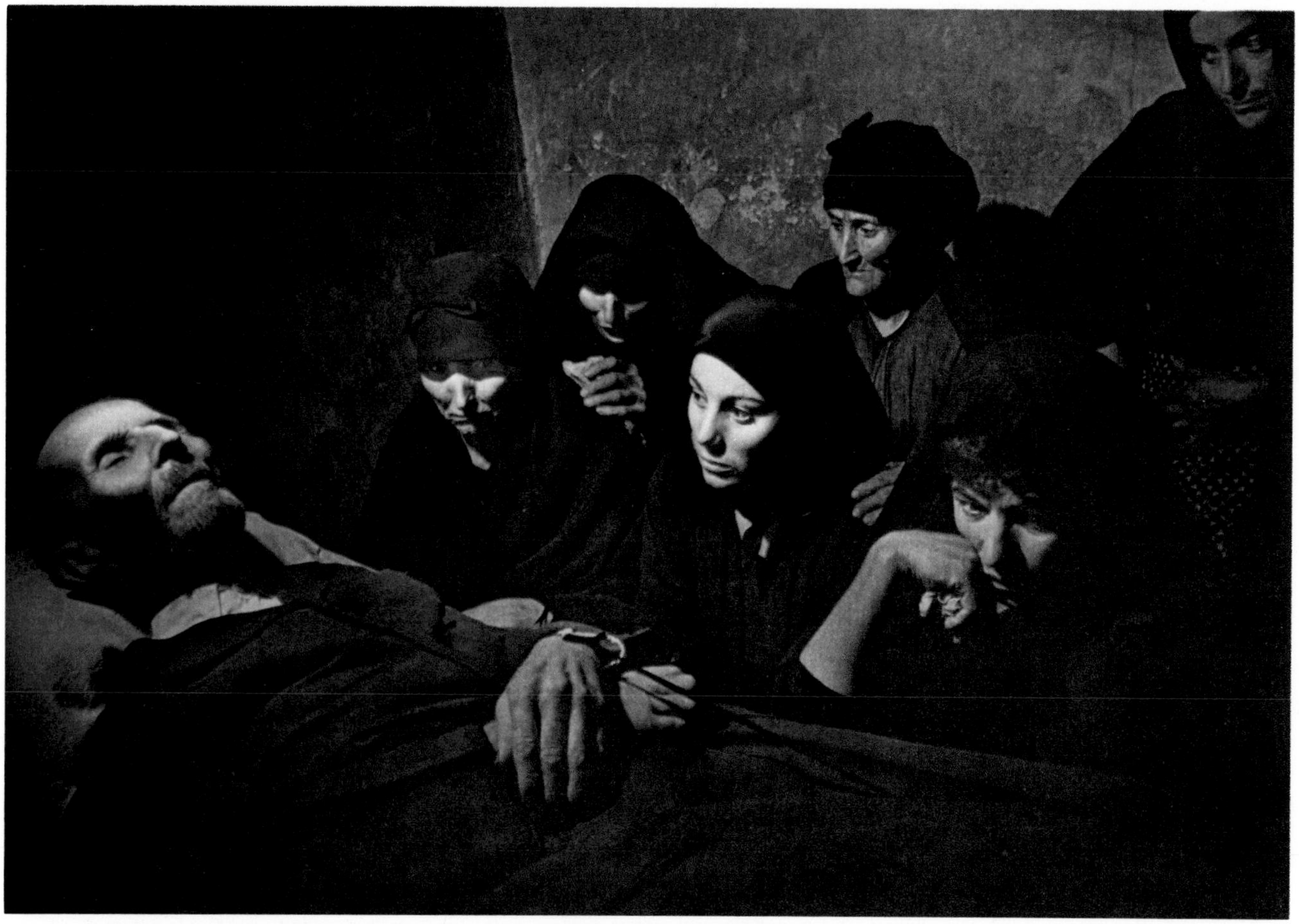

Figure 6: DEATH SCENE

Figure 7: SCHWEITZER WITH THE LEPER

Figure 8: SCHWEITZER AT HIS DESK

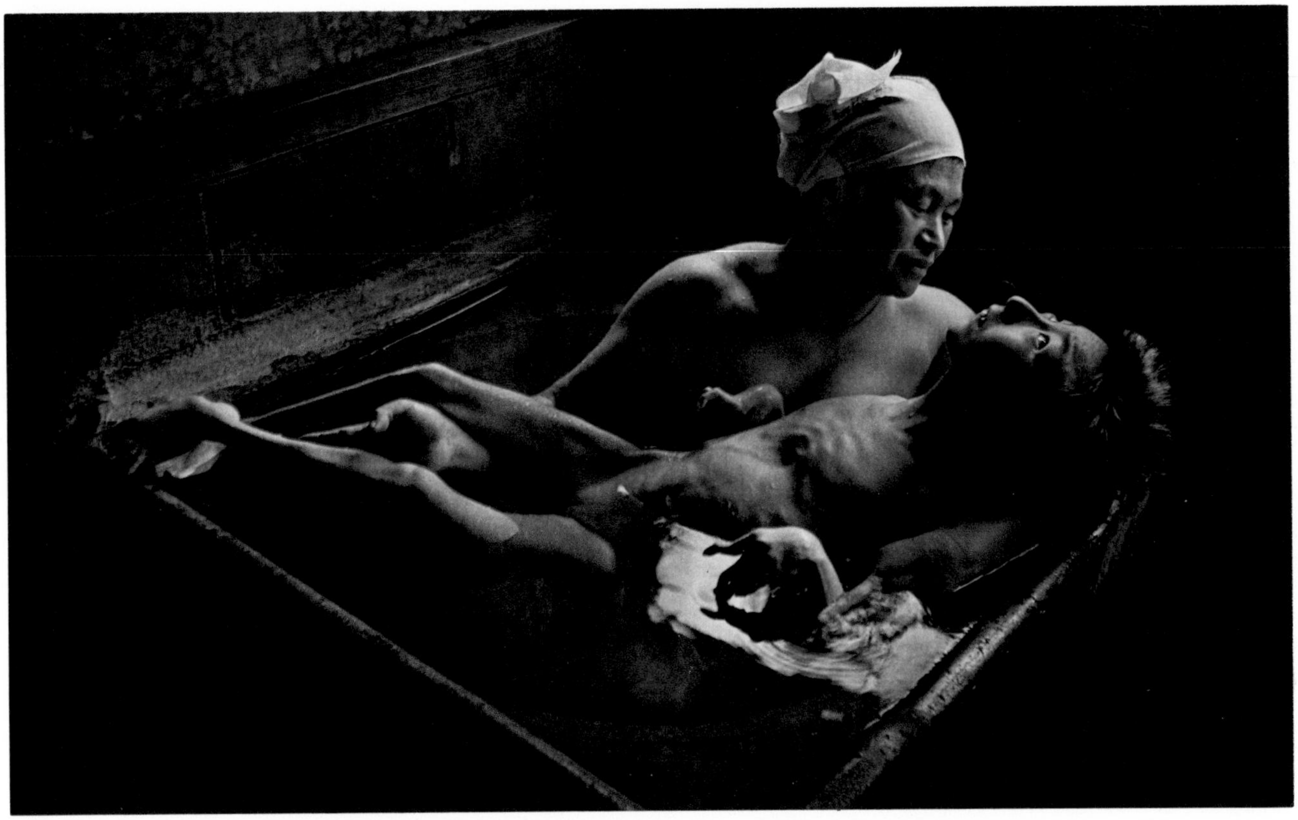

Figure 9: TOMOKO IN THE BATH (before dodging and burning)

Figure 10: TOMOKO IN THE BATH

GEORGE TICE

George Tice was born in Newark, New Jersey, in 1938. He majored in commercial photography at the Newark Vocational and Technical High School, leaving it to become a darkroom assistant.

A year later he joined the Navy, as an official photographer. After his Navy service, he photographed the Pennsylvania Dutch. This culminated in 1970 with the publication of his first book, FIELDS OF PEACE (Doubleday, New York).

In 1967 Tice commenced work on a photographic portrait of Paterson, New Jersey. PATERSON was published in 1971 (Rutgers University Press, New Brunswick, New Jersey) and was awarded the Grand Prix du Festival d'Arles as the best photography book of the year. GOODBYE, RIVER, GOODBYE also came out in 1971 (Doubleday, New York). Two years later, Tice received a National Endowment for the Arts grant and a Guggenheim Fellowship to work on URBAN LANDSCAPES: A NEW JERSEY PORTRAIT (Rutgers University Press, New Brunswick, New Jersey). His book SEACOAST MAINE (Doubleday, New York) followed in 1973.

A monograph of his photographs, GEORGE A. TICE, PHOTOGRAPHER, was published in 1975 by Rutgers University Press in conjunction with a retrospective exhibition held at The Witkin Gallery, New York.

Tice teaches a master class in photography at the New School for Social Research in New York.

Selected one-man shows:

1969: The Witkin Gallery, New York

1970: 831 Gallery, Birmingham, Alabama

1971: Art Institute of Chicago

1972: Metropolitan Museum of Art, New York

1973: The Witkin Gallery, New York

1975: The Witkin Gallery, New York

Selected collections:
Museum of Modern Art, New York
Metropolitan Museum of Art, New York
Bibliothèque Nationale, Paris
Library of Congress, Washington, D.C.
Victoria and Albert Museum, London

> Every photographer who has the good and advancement of photography at heart, should feel indebted to Mr. Willis for placing within his power a process by which he is able to produce work comparable, on artistic grounds, with any black and white process. We have no hesitation in saying that the discovery and subsequent practice of this process has had an incalculable amount of influence in raising the standard of photography. No artist could rest content to practice photography alone as an art, so long as such inartistic printing methods as the pre-platinotype processes were in vogue. If the photogravure process and the platinotype process were to become lost arts, we, for our part, should never take another photograph.

These words of foreboding are from Peter Henry Emerson's textbook, NATURALISTIC PHOTOGRAPHY, published in 1889. The platinotype process has in fact become photography's lost art. Over the years, I've come across numerous references to platinum paper, praising its intrinsic beauty and mourning its passing. Born into this chlorobromide era and feeling deprived, I consoled myself with the thought that silver printing paper might not be available to photographers of the future. I was fortunate to be able to work in silver. Lurking in my mind, however, was the thought that even though platinum paper is no longer manufactured, why couldn't I prepare papers myself and limit printing to selected photographs appropriate to the process?

After seeing a large collection of Frederick H. Evans' photographs in platinum, I decided to pursue it. I was deeply moved by Evans' work. It approaches the unattainable: perfection in both camera work and printmaking.

Evans, in the AMATEUR PHOTOGRAPHER of 1910, states:

> As photographers we should, I think, feel ourselves bound to print every negative that will permit in platinotype, the medium that will best, most innocently and completely render its subtle tones and gradations, that will best exhibit the photography of the photograph . . . It is a thousand pities that platinotype is not controllable without loss of purity in surface and texture. Control of the negative by preparing for printing is never successful in the degree requisite for photographic perfection; the photography is altered, its purity is impaired, its gradations falsified . . . .

William Willis, an Englishman, credited with the invention of the process in 1873, manufactured it under the name "Platinotype." There were two methods of processing, hot and cold bath, with papers made for each. It was available in black and white or sepia, rough and smooth, and as cut sheets or rolls. Being extremely hygroscopic, the paper did not keep well and had to be packaged in tins containing a lump of calcium chloride to absorb moisture. The process reached such a high degree of perfection that some felt the paper had to be properly mellowed. They purposely removed the chemical lump months before using it. This would slightly degrade the tonal quality of the platinum print.

The chief sources of platinum lie in South America, Russia and Canada. At the time that Willis invented the process, platinum was an inexpensive metal. During the early gold-mining days in California, platinum was not even considered worth saving, but by 1906 its value had risen and continues to do so. In 1916 the British government forbade the use of platinum for photography since the now precious metal was needed for the war effort. The manufacturer, seeking a substitute, brought out Satista and Satoid. These papers utilized a combination of platinum and silver. Later, palladium, a less expensive metal of the platinum group, was substituted, and this paper was marketed under the name Palladiotype.

After World War I platinum papers were again on the market. Because of their cost and the popularity of other papers, they were rarely used. In 1938 they became unavailable.

What are the characteristics of a platinum print (Figure10) as opposed to the contemporary chlorobromide print (Figure 11)? Platinum prints have an absolutely matte surface. There is no glare from any angle of viewing. A developed and cleared print consists of very fine particles of metallic platinum spread throughout the fibers of the paper. There is no emulsion as such, and once flattened, the print will remain flat, eliminating the need for mounting. Platinum, a contact printing process which is partially printed out in sunlight and fully developed out, is capable of reproducing a very long tonal scale. The self-masking of the shadows, characteristic of all printing out processes, permits the subtle highlight values to register without the shadows blocking up. When a negative is printed, the shadows are the first to show on the paper. The top layer of the "emulsion" darkens, acting as a mask. It holds back light so that the shadow will not get as dark as it would in a silver print which is developed out. Light can pass through the dense highlights without the shadows going black, making for luminous shadow detail.

The unique beauty of a soft, full-scale platinum print is its real value, but there are also other advantages. Platinum is a more stable metal than silver. Platinum prints are considered to be as permanent as the paper on which the image rests. A greater variety of paper surfaces and tints is available. Print color and mount color can be matched perfectly by mounting on the same paper as that sensitized. A light-tight darkroom is not essential. All the steps of sensitizing and developing can be accomplished in indirect existing light. Contrast is easily controlled by varying the proportions of the sensitizer solutions.

The chief disadvantage of working in platinum is its cost. Also, it is impossible to enlarge directly since it is a contact process and, therefore, a large or enlarged negative is necessary. While the process is basically simple, it is time-consuming and laborious. The controls of dodging and burning are not practical because of the relatively long printing exposures. However, these controls can be employed in the making of an enlarged negative.

To make a platinum print, the first item you need is a negative the size you want the print to be. Large view camera work is ideal in conjunction with this process. If you use a small hand camera, an enlarged negative can be made by projecting the negative on film, then contact printing the positive onto another sheet of film. For this purpose I recommend Kodak Professional Copy Film.

CHEMICALS FOR SENSITIZER:
potassium chloroplatinite (K_2PtCl_4)
ferric oxalate
oxalic acid
potassium chlorate
distilled water

CHEMICALS FOR PROCESSING:
potassium oxalate, neutral (1 lb.)
hydrochloric acid, c.p. (1 pt.)

MATERIALS: (Figure 1)
balance scale
sunlamp
contact printing frame
camel hair brush, 1 inch long (coat the metal ferrule and base hairs with household cement)
push-pins
small glass jigger
glass graduate (2 oz.)
glass stirring rod
amber bottles (for developer and clearing bath storage)
three 2 oz. amber bottles with minim droppers (for sensitizer)
plywood board (large enough to tack paper to be sensitized)
four trays (for processing)
large tray (for washing)

My favorite paper is Crane's writing paper, AS-8111, pearl white, kid finish. Crane's papers are 100 percent rag and can be ordered in 8½x11 sheets. Some papers are inappropriate, being too rough in texture or too absorbent. Others need to be sized before sensitizing, and some simply do not work. On Strathmore papers, for instance, an ugly granulated image will result.

The Rives Paper Company has recently introduced a new paper especially manufactured for the hand-sensitized platinum process. It is called "Rives Platinotype." The sheets are fully sized and measure 19½x25½. The paper is available through Andrews/Nelson/Whitehead, 31-10 48th Avenue, Long Island City, N.Y. 11101.

These three stock solutions are required to prepare the sensitizing mixture:

1. distilled water (125 F) — 1 oz.
oxalic acid — 8 grains
ferric oxalate — 120 grains

2. distilled water (125 F) — 1 oz.
oxalic acid — 8 grains
ferric oxalate — 120 grains
potassium chlorate — 2 grains

3. distilled water (125 F) — 2⅜ oz.
potassium chloroplatinite — 219½ grains

Palladium may be substituted for platinum by using 156 grains sodium chloropalladite ($NaPdCl_4$) to 2⅜ oz. distilled water for solution 3.

After mixing the three solutions separately in glass graduates, pour each into an amber bottle and label them 1, 2, and 3. Solution 2 contains potassium chlorate, which increases the contrast of the print. You can control contrast by varying the amounts of each stock solution used in your sensitizing mixture:

A: FOR VERY SOFT PRINTS
No. 1 22 minims
No. 2 0 minims
No. 3 24 minims

B: FOR SOFT PRINTS
No. 1 18 minims
No. 2 4 minims
No. 3 24 minims

C: FOR AVERAGE PRINTS

No. 1	14 minims
No. 2	8 minims
No. 3	24 minims

D: FOR CONTRASTY PRINTS

No. 1	10 minims
No. 2	12 minims
No. 3	24 minims

E: FOR VERY CONTRASTY PRINTS

No. 1	0 minims
No. 2	22 minims
No. 3	24 minims

The above dilutions are measured into a small glass jigger with a dropper, one minim being one drop (Figure 2). Mix with a stirring rod and pour the solution onto a sheet of paper which has been tacked at four corners to a board held flat, not upright (Figure 3). The brush should be dampened with water before spreading the sensitizer. Brush horizontally, then vertically, until the liquid has been spread evenly over the surface of the paper (Figure 4). This should be done rapidly, being completed before the sensitizer begins to dry. Otherwise the results will show patchy brushstrokes. The 46 minims of sensitizer will coat an 8½x11 sheet of paper.

Rinse the brush and jigger thoroughly after sensitizing. Hang the sensitized paper by a corner and allow it to dry in a darkened room for ten minutes. The paper will be surface dry. Do not remove any brush hairs that might have stuck to the paper surface until the paper is completely dry.

Continue the drying process by holding the paper over a gas burner or hotplate, sensitized side up, until the paper is bone dry (Figure 5). At this stage the paper will crackle when flexed. It will also take on a deeper yellow-orange color. Be careful not to scorch the sensitizer during drying.

The paper is now ready for printing. Trim it to the size of the negative and use the excess for tests. Set the negative and sensitized paper into the printing frame, and place under a sunlamp at a distance of 24 inches (Figure 6). (Sunlight may be used, but for consistency of exposure a sunlamp is preferable.) Expose strips for twenty, twenty-five, and thirty minutes as a trial. The exposed strip may be viewed by indirect light, which will reveal a partially printed yellow-gray image. The sensitizer I use most often is the C solution with exposures averaging about twenty-five minutes. The lamp can be brought closer for smaller negatives.

Mix one pound of potassium oxalate in 48 ounces of water. The temperature of this solution should be no less

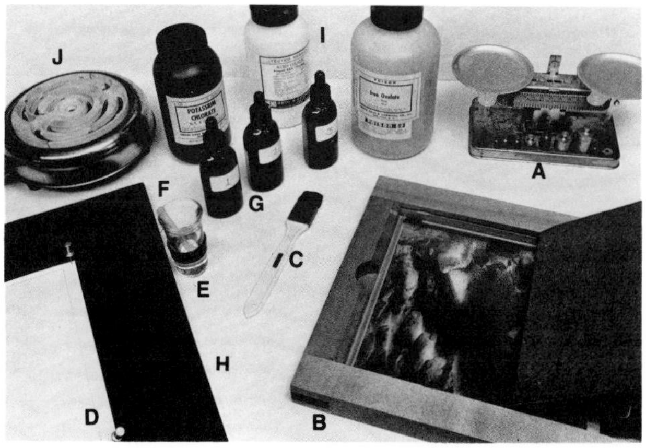

Figure 1.

A: Balance scale B: Contact printing frame C: Camel hair brush D: Pushpins E: Glass jigger F: Glass stirring rod G: 2 oz. amber bottles with minim droppers H: Plywood board I: Chemicals J: Hot plate

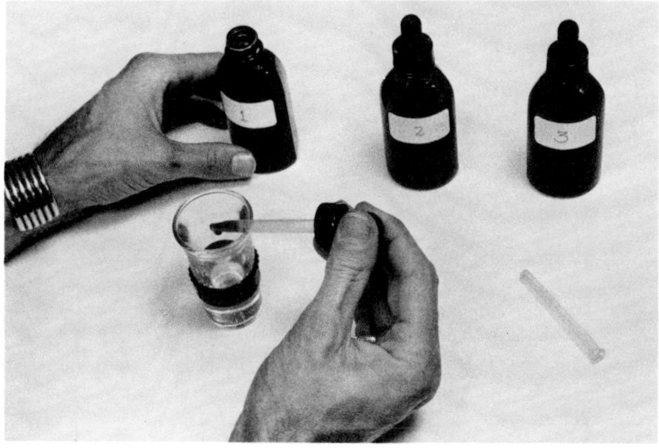

Figure 2.

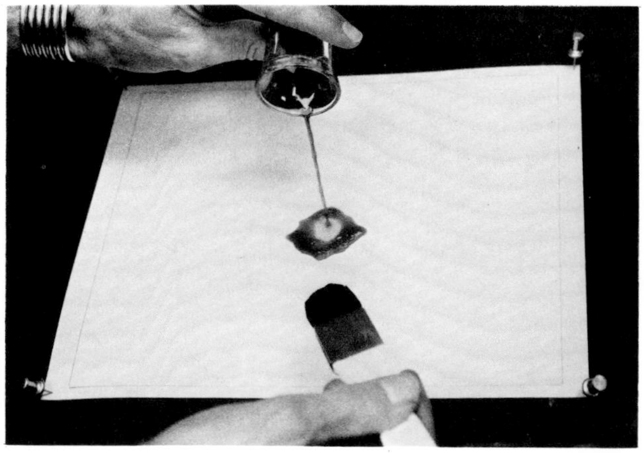

Figure 3.

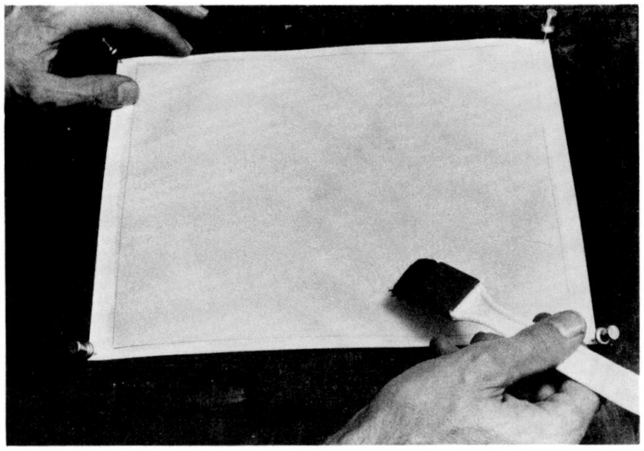

Figure 4.

Figure 5.

Figure 6.

than 60 F. The higher the temperature, the warmer the image color. Place the exposed print face up in a tray with this developer as you would to develop a conventional print (Figure 7). Stop any air bubbles that have formed on the surface with your finger. Development is complete after a few seconds, but continue to develop for two minutes. The developer can be used indefinitely, with occasional filtering and adding of fresh developer to bring up the level.

Prepare three solutions of hydrochloric acid diluted 1:60 with water. The print should remain in each bath for five minutes, and then be washed for twenty minutes. After each session, discard the third bath. The other two clearing baths can be saved, but a fresh first bath should always be used.

After washing, gently place the delicate wet print face down on a clean, hard surface and carefully blot with a clean white towel. Turn the print over and blot again (Figure 8). As it air dries, the print will darken and become colder in tone. Adjustments in contrast and exposure must be based on the dried print. After drying, the print can be flattened under pressure. Use black India ink diluted with water for spotting, as it matches the warm black of a platinum print perfectly.

Figure 10 is a print from an 8x10 negative I made of the Roaring Fork River in Aspen, Colorado. It was taken after sunset using a 300mm lens. The exposure was one second between *f*/22 and *f*/32. Actually I took two exposures, one at one second and one at ten seconds. One second is perfect here because it reveals just enough movement, yet there is also a certain amount of detail in the tracings of the moving water. At ten seconds, all that highlight detail is lost and the whole thing looks as if dry ice had been thrown into the river. It would become quite a different image again if I had used a fast shutter speed and stopped the moving water.

The film is Tri-X, which I always use. Even working outdoors in bright sun, if you want complete depth of field, you have to stop down. This means much slower shutter speeds, so I find a fast film essential.

I tray develop one or two negatives at a time for five minutes in straight D-76, heating the developer to 75 F. That's the warmest temperature you can develop at, and the shortest developing time. This way I spend a minimum amount of time in the darkroom developing film. However, if I were using 35mm film with this high a developer temperature, I might get too much grain on enlargement. With the 8x10 negative, grain isn't a consideration. Even 20x24 enlargements are grainless.

The ideal 8x10 negative has an entirely different character from a 35mm negative. A 35mm negative should be more transparent. If you overexpose too much, you lose sharpness and add grain. With an 8x10 negative, you can expose much more fully so that there are no areas of clear transparency, just detail throughout.

In the print of the negative (Figure 9) you can see the amount of detail even in the shadows. Actually, there is even more detail than I could show, but it gives you an idea of what an 8x10 negative suitable for platinum printing looks like. It has a full tonal scale. It goes the whole range from the transparency of the shadows to the high density of the water highlights. Perhaps I could have exposed even more fully with complete shadow detail and denser highlights, but then I would not have been able to print this negative on conventional silver printing paper.

I try to make a negative I can print on both a conventional chlorobromide paper and a platinum paper as well. If I wanted to take full advantage of the platinum medium, I would make negatives that would print on a zero grade paper. You can print a very long scale of tones in platinum that would be much too contrasty in silver. Platinum prints are always softer in contrast than silver prints.

In making the platinum print of this negative, I used the C sensitizer, the one for normal contrast. One way to tell what degree of contrast a negative requires is to test the negative on chlorobromide paper and see what grade is suitable. The C sensitizer is equivalent to a No. 2 paper.

Next, I made my test strips to determine the exposure time. In this case it turned out to be twenty-five minutes. Although burning in is extremely tedious in platinum, I did edge burn the right side of this print a bit and did some local burning in as well. This involved holding a piece of cardboard with a hole in it over the contact printing frame for several minutes. The development, clearing, washing, and drying proceeded as explained above.

In making the silver print (Figure 11), I put the negative and paper into the contact printing frame and used the enlarger as a light source. My favorite paper is Brovira. I also use Portriga, Rapid Kodabromide, Portralure M, and sometimes Ilford semimatte finish. Here I used Brovira No. 2.

An average exposure on a normal grade of paper might be, say, six seconds, and burning in might be around eighteen seconds. Figure 11 is not a straight print. It required some local burning in of the white water in the top portion of the negative to get a little more highlight detail. And, of course, parts of the edges required burning in, for example, the rocks in the upper-right-hand corner and along the right edge. In developing roll film on reels, you build up density around the edges, but with tray developed sheet film, the process doesn't create this buildup. There is, however, always a certain pictorial imbalance in natural lighting. If the left edge of an image is closer to the sun, it's going to be lighter than the right edge. Sometimes it's a question of making the edges a little softer by darkening them. This makes

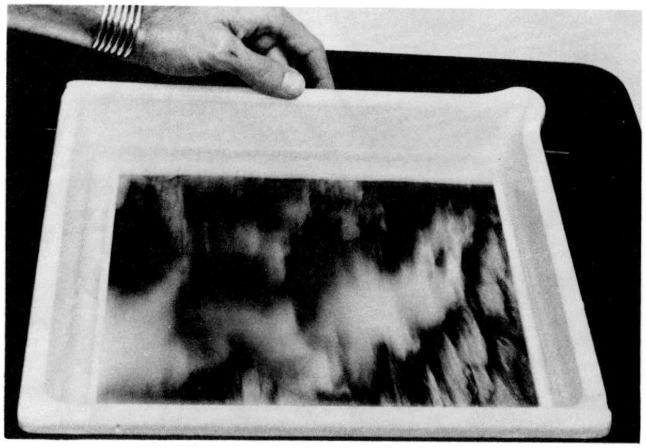

Figure 7.

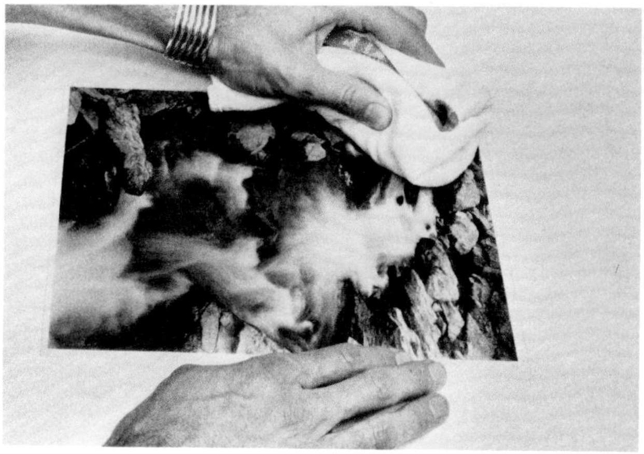

Figure 8.

Figure 9 (reproduced smaller than original negative)

the center of the picture brighter and contains the eye of the viewer. Although edge burning is very subtle, it sometimes turns a little slice of something into a picture.

I think photography is perfected enough so that most things can be printed straight, except for a little edge burning. I never do any dodging because I never underexpose my film. There are no thin shadows to hold back. My procedures are simple. I use one developer for all formats of film, D-76, and one developer for all prints (except platinum), Dektol. I dilute this paper developer 1:2 and develop prints for two minutes.

There are times when I will develop longer or dilute the developer more to control contrast to the half grade. If a negative seems too soft on No. 2, and to go to a No. 3 would be too drastic a jump, I take a No. 2 paper and increase the development time (decreasing the exposure time) or use a more concentrated stock solution. By overdeveloping that print, for four minutes, the contrast is increased by a half grade. This should be done with the print face down in the tray so that the safelight doesn't start to fog it. It is very important to agitate the print constantly while it is in the developer in order to get maximum contrast and full, even action of the chemicals.

The print then goes into the stop bath. I use an ounce and a half of 28% acetic acid to a quart of water, leaving the print in the stop bath until I feel the slippery alkaline developer dissolve, which takes about fifteen to twenty seconds.

Then the print goes into the fixer. I use two baths of five minutes each. After hypo-clearing and toning, I wash the print and air dry it on a fiberglass screen. When it is completely dry, I place it between mounts and put it face down into the dry mount press at 225 F for about ten seconds and then let it cool. By drying it face down, you reverse the natural tendency of paper to curl toward the emulsion.

I've been photographing for twenty-two years. During much of this time my printing was haphazard. I think that in making a print, the procedure itself isn't so difficult, but the critical decisions are. Being able to look at a test print and know where you want it to go, darker or lighter, more contrasty or softer. That's the crucial ability that takes a certain number of years to develop.

FILM	ASA RATING	DEVELOPER	SOLUTION & TIME	AGITATION
Tri-X: 8x10	200	D-76 75 F	Full strength 5 minutes	Continuous Tray development

ENLARGER	LENS	LIGHT SOURCE	USUAL APERTURE	USUAL EXPOSURE
Unidentifiable hand made 8x10	Goerz Apochromat Artar 10¾ inch *f*/9.5	Aristo cold light head	*f*/32	12 seconds for 16 x 20 prints

PAPER	DEVELOPER	SOLUTION & TIME	STOP BATH	FIXER
Brovira III Nos. 1 to 4	Dektol	1:2 2 to 3 minutes	28% glacial acetic acid solution 20 seconds	Kodak F-5 2 baths 5 minutes in each

WASH	TONING	DRYING	FLATTENING	PRESENTATION
3 minutes hypo clearing bath 45 minutes archival print washer	Selenium 1:12 2 to 10 minutes	Air dry on fiberglass screen	Sandwiched between museum boards in drymount press at 225F for 10 seconds	Drymount on museum board

Figure 10: ROARING FORK RIVER (platinum print)

Figure 11: ROARING FORK RIVER (chlorobromide print)

JERRY N. UELSMANN

Jerry N. Uelsmann was born in Detroit in 1934. In 1953 he entered The Rochester Institute of Technology and studied with Ralph Hattersley and Minor White. He received his BFA in 1957 and was first published in the PHOTOGRAPHY ANNUAL of that year. He attended Indiana University, where he studied with Henry Holmes Smith, earning his MFA. In 1960 he joined the faculty of the University of Florida in Gainesville. Uelsmann was awarded a Guggenheim Fellowship in 1967.

In 1971 the Aperture Monograph, JERRY N. UELSMANN, was published. A second edition was released in 1973, the year he was appointed a Fellow of The Royal Photographic Society of Great Britain.

He received a Faculty Development Grant from the University of Florida in 1971 and a National Endowment for the Arts grant in 1972. In 1975 SILVER MEDITATIONS (Morgan and Morgan, Dobbs Ferry, New York) was published.

Uelsmann is a Graduate Research Professor at the University of Florida, Gainesville.

Selected one-man shows:

1967: Museum of Modern Art, New York

1968: Creative Photography Gallery, Massachusetts Institute of Technology, Cambridge

1970: George Eastman House, Rochester, New York

1972: The Witkin Gallery, New York

1973: 831 Gallery, Birmingham, Alabama

1974: American Cultural Center, Paris

1975: Rochester Institute of Technology, Rochester, New York

Selected collections:
Smithsonian Institution, Washington, D.C.
Boston Museum of Fine Arts
Metropolitan Museum of Art, New York
National Gallery of Canada, Ottawa
Victoria and Albert Museum, London
Royal Photographic Society of Great Britain, London
Bibliothèque Nationale, Paris

Diane Farris

Basically, I was brought up in the straight tradition. I had the opportunity to study with Minor White. I was taught the Zone System. Working in that manner for many years, I found that I became restless. I began to apply a sort of overthink when taking a picture. All these decisions would be floating around in my head. I found I could talk myself out of anything. The tremendous search for an image that meant something became more and more discouraging. I would look at my proof sheets and know why I took a certain picture, but it never seemed to be a complete image. Multiple printing solved this problem.

How you actually get started is difficult to pinpoint, but accidental things happen and you wonder and experiment. My first multiple print was across the frame where there was a natural black. I had already played around with the idea of multiple printing as a student, and I gradually got more and more into the idea of altering the image in process. After graduate school, for many years I was the only photographer in the art department at the University of Florida. The people in the other media were all talking about in process discovery. For instance, the painter doesn't begin with a fully conceived canvas. He or she allows for a kind of dialogue. Listening to people with this attitude led me to question the idea that the moment of creation takes place with the camera and that you become a craftsman in the darkroom to bring the camera vision into being. It doesn't matter at what point the image is realized, as long as it happens. I truly believe that the quality of the moment which we traditionally associate with the camera experience can be very much a part of the darkroom experience also.

I like the idea of mystery and enigma, of catering to accident. You know your materials, but they themselves have to have a voice in the process. When I'm at my worst, I run things through a prescribed ritual. It's like juggling. When I'm at my best, I can develop a very nice relationship with an image as it emerges. I listen to what it's telling me and begin with just the barest of clues to see what might work, what might happen. It's very important to have a playful attitude toward process, a constant willingness to try any alternative you can conceive. Of course you have to evaluate, but you must avoid being too critical at any point. One of the problems in the university situation is that students frequently think too much. You can kill any idea in its embryonic stage, when an image is just starting to develop its own life. But if you work with an idea long enough, it somehow takes on a life system of its own that must be acknowledged.

There are many attitudes that must be resolved before you can be free with the process. Experimentation involves inventing a language at the same time you're using it. Of necessity, you make some asinine statements, but you have to do this. It's part of the joy and the mystery. I've allowed a little more irreverence and absurdity to sneak into my work these past few years.

If you work with a post-visualization approach, you have access to your entire visual heritage. Anything you have photographed now becomes part of your collective consciousness, so it's essential that you establish a simple filing system. I make proof sheets of everything and then take the negatives and put them in a regular business envelope with the end cut off. These are numbered. (An example might be number 3, April 1975.) Then I put the same number on the back of the proof sheet. The negatives are kept in numerical order, but I let the proof sheets get mixed up. I have found that I can pick up a hundred proof sheets and in a matter of five minutes find the particular image I want to work with. Then I go to the negative filing system and locate the matching negative. Another phenomenon that has to be accommodated by any filing system is that often half way through a particular image I may remember a negative I made four years earlier and I have to have a rapid way of finding it. The flow must continue. I want a process whereby I can see change quickly. I'm not able to work with a system that involves waiting a couple of days to see the results of some decision and then trying something else. I need a retrievable system that is not complex, one that includes a very loose structure for proof sheets. They are my visual dictionary and/or diary. These photographs represent everything that I've seen and responded to.

Because of the way I work, a lot of my proof sheets involve the collecting of things visually. When I photograph, I think I have more options than most photographers. If I see an image that is visually cohesive and I sense that camera moment, I can take the photograph. At the same time, I collect fragments that I respond to. They might later become part of something I would call a meaningful image. A simple thing like a piece of paper blowing in the wind might serve as the foreground of an image yet to be realized. I rarely decide while I'm taking the photograph where the element will end up. Sometimes it's obvious that a particular old house might serve as a background or a particular rock form might work in the foreground. But most of the time I've no real knowledge of where it's going to end up. When shooting, the only technical adjustment I might make is to leave a little more space at the top of the negative where something is obviously a foreground subject and, where it will be a background, a little space at the bottom. This technique permits multiple blending of images.

I shoot 2¼. You can blend images with a 35mm format, but by combining the 2¼ squares you tend to get a more natural rectangle. I also like the idea that I don't have to

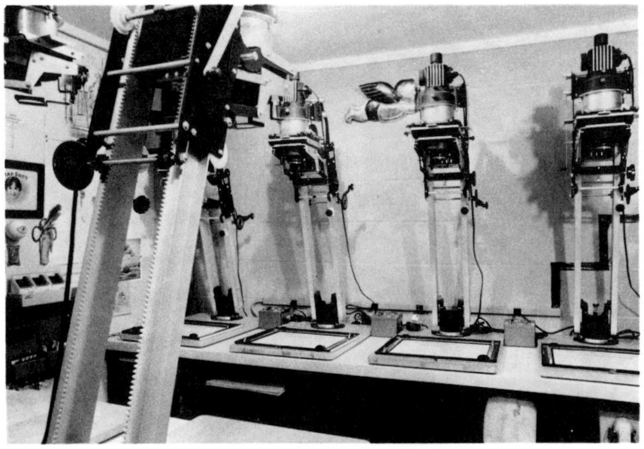

Figure 1.

Figure 2.

make decisions about horizontal versus vertical at the point of shooting a photograph.

When I need additional speed, I shoot with Tri-X, but for the most part I use Plus-X and process the film in Microdol-X, one to three, at 75 F for ten and one half minutes. Microdol gives a softer negative; if you get involved in negative sandwiching (putting two negatives together in the enlarger), it will build up less density than a more contrasty developer, so you can print a more complete tonal range.

When I'm going to print, I like to set aside a large block of time. I'm not a photographer who likes to pop into the darkroom for a couple of hours. I like comfortable conditions and feel that this is extremely important. One of my theories as to why more photographers have not worked with darkroom process is that their darkrooms are often versions of the black hole of Calcutta. My new darkroom is a pleasure. It has carpeting on the floor and a hi-fi. The water is temperature controlled. This is a place where I can spend eight or ten hours without feeling the least bit claustrophobic. I'm not always in there for that long, but my point is that the darkroom should be comfortable (Figure 1).

In the photo magazines the emphasis is on the camera end of the process. Many photographers have five or six cameras. They usually have only one enlarger, frequently a Tinker Toy B22 with palsy in its brace system. I have many enlargers that aid in the multiple printing process, but I have only one camera, the Bronica with a couple of lenses.

When I get ready to print, I sit down with a stack of proof sheets. Usually the things that are most recent are on top, but they get rapidly mixed with the others. I look at these proof sheets and try to find clues to things that might work together (Figure 2). Sometimes (and this is a mental state) I'll sit down and in half an hour I can make more little notes of things I want to try than I could possibly do in a week. Other times I'll sit down and look at the proof sheets and think, "What the hell am I doing in photography? This is nowhere."

Here are four proof sheets. I was intrigued by the large rock form in proof sheet Figure 3A. It's like an egg. I could see it as a possible foreground, but I didn't know where it belonged. I fold this proof sheet and then go on to other sheets where I discover the banyan tree in Figure 3B. I wonder how it would look with the rock. When I'm working things out, I usually begin with a simple blend, a foreground and background, for instance. It could be diagonal or horizontal, but I look for a common blending surface. This doesn't have to actually be of the same material. The upper part of the rock image is rock ledge and the lower part of the banyan tree image is leaves and grass, but the two have a tonal and textural cohesiveness that makes blending possible. I see two images and the similar texture and tonal quality and I

Figure 3A

Figure 3B

Figure 3C

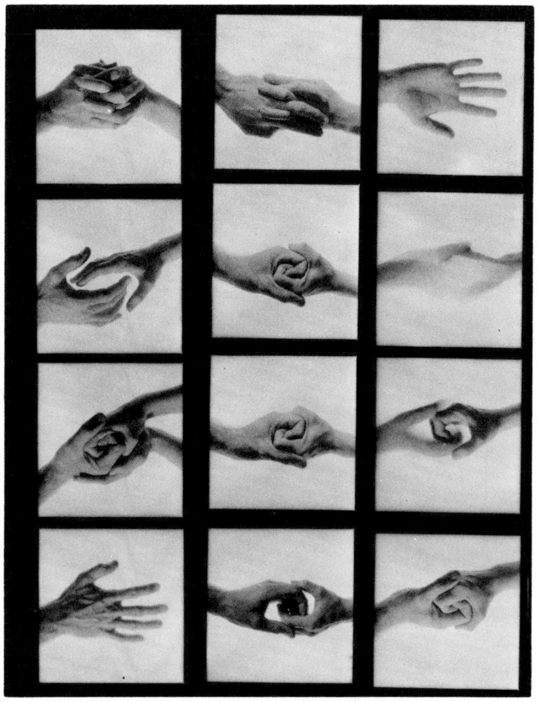

Figure 3D

think, "That's kind of interesting, that rock played up against that tree." Then I make a little note of the combination and move on to the next possibility.

I don't get too emotionally involved in the image at this point. It's just something to try. Still working with this rock, I go through some other proof sheets. As I look at them, it occurs to me that the rock and the mountains might work well together.

The reason for these alternatives is that you can't know how the image is going to work out until you get into the darkroom and do it. I love the idea that you begin with clues, suggestions, possibilities. When the image finally surfaces in the developer, it's sometimes a disaster; other times you know you're onto something. You have to listen to what the image is saying at this point. I couldn't decide between these two versions, so I tried them both.

My darkroom technique in this print is relatively simple. I put the foreground negative, the rock, into the enlarger (Figures 4 and 5). I put the background negative, the mountains, into a second enlarger (Figure 6). It's important to have some accurate system of placing the paper. I use Saunders easels. The papers I use are Polycontrast or Varilour VLTW. I like some of the other papers better, but I need the variable contrast because different negatives may require different grades of contrast. Also, when you're blending regular negatives, you frequently have to increase the contrast slightly. On the other hand, if you're working with a negative sandwich, two negatives in the same carrier, you usually need to lower the contrast. Where this process can grow incredibly is when you start combining techniques, for instance, the foreground might be a negative sandwich. Then you would need a low contrast filter to hold any kind of tone in your highlights and shadows. Your background might be a normal negative, and then you would usually need either no filter or a slight increase in contrast.

Figure 4.

The developer I use is LPD by Ethol and I think it's really fine. It's supposed to have a longer tray life and low fog level. But I hestiate to make a big thing out of it because when I go around the country doing demonstrations I use whatever is available and I get the same kind of print. You want a developer with a low fog level so that you can leave paper in it for three or four minutes without it screwing up too much.

In Figure 5, you see what happens when I print just the foreground negative. Initially, I used to block out the top part of the paper by dodging with a card so that the image fades off into pure white. Using the hand held card was crazy because for every one I got, I screwed up five others. What I do now is place a piece of cardboard on a filter holder immediately below the enlarger lens (Figure 4). As you stop down the lens, this edge will become sharper, but you want

Figure 5.

Figure 6.

Figure 7.

Figure 8.

to keep it soft. It provides a relatively soft edge around *f*/8 or *f*/11, which helps the two images come together. Then I make a crude little sketch on the back of an old print to indicate where this soft edge occurs. I go to the second enlarger and set up my background negative. In Figure 6 you can see just the mountains alone. I focus the negative and, using my sketch, I try to line it up above the rock image, allowing for about an inch of overlap. You see the area of overlap by comparing Figures 7 and 8 where the two images are coming together. It is important that you allow for this transitional space. I call this technique "blending," blending one image with another.

A common problem that people experience is getting the tone between the two images even. If the tone is too light, that means the areas have not overlapped enough, and if it's too dark, they've overlapped too much. On occasion you can't let them overlap much because part of one image may eat into part of another image where you don't want it to. In this case you simply have to burn in the overlapped area, but you must do your blocking close to the lens because if either edge gets too hard there's no way to camouflage it. The joy, and I suppose the sophistication, of working with this technique over the years is that you realize how many things that seemingly would not come together develop a visual cohesiveness photographically.

I have shown with Figures 7 and 8 how two negatives can be successfully blended to form a single image. At this point I looked at the image for a while in the fixer and I thought something more could happen to it. I felt it could become a little more complex and I began considering what possibilities I had. The only area that was still a bit light was the rock itself. Even though there's tone in the rock, that area of the paper can still receive an additional image. Working with multiple printing, you become very conscious of lights and darks as you photograph. For instance, you realize that a white building in a photograph provides a form which could have something printed on it later.

About five years ago the idea occurred to me to photograph on a lightbox so that I would have a pure white background. Objects could then be printed into various areas without much tehnical hassle. Figure 3D is of twelve photographs of hands taken over a lightbox. A lightbox, as you surely know, is simply that — a box containing lights under a ground glass, which gives you an even, light background. There is light shining onto the hands as well as light from the box, but the backlight is stronger so that you build up a nice even density. I looked at many proof sheets, but the only one that seemed to have a possibility for success was Figure 9. I first tried a fist form, which didn't work, and then decided to try the open hands.

Now I go to a third enlarger, set up the hands negative, and try to line them up to project onto the rock form. I still soften the edges of this image by printing through a hole in a card, because even though you have a pure white background, some light is bound to come through. If the hard edges aren't dodged, they will show. You might not even be able to see it in the darkroom and yet when the print dries, there it is, a real bummer.

To my delight and amazement, these hands fit perfectly into the rock form. The details of these alignments are some of the synchronistic events that are messages from the interior. The thumb on the right happens to line up with a crack in the rock. Another interesting thing is that behind the rock there is a darker tonality, so that while in reality the hand does not end at the edge of the rock, this darker surface creates the illusion that the rock is contained within the hand and vice versa. The first hands I tried to print looked as if they were painted onto the rock. I shifted to the hands I ended up using and tried various sizes. Once I got the size used in Figure 10 the hand became the rock. Were the hands on the rock, part of the rock? Is the rock the hands? It's a circular thing. I like this little visual enigma.

Another intriguing element about working this way is that it's like having a magician explain everything and finding out that the magic is still there. There's no camouflage, nothing is happening in the shadows. The image is technically precise, photographically speaking, but at the same time, the mystery and ambiguity remain.

When you start using many negatives for an image (Figure 10 involves three), there is a problem of a slight fog building up. The print will tend to get a little softer than I would like. Sometimes I can compensate for this by increasing the contrast, but sometimes I have to settle for it.

At this point, if I like the image, I try to run an edition. The joy for me is getting there, so I'm really bad about this last part. I usually make about six prints. One advantage to this last step is that I have more sustained contact with the image. As I continue to look at it, my mind begins to consider what else can happen, how it could change. It occurred to me that maybe I could work this same rock form in with another background. I had considered the rock in relation to the banyan tree background earlier. I simply leave the negatives for the rock and hands in their enlargers and get the negative of the banyan tree. As shown in Figure 11, I do some changing of scale with the enlargers so that the tree blends with the foreground rock and they come together to form a cohesive image. I made a print, Figure 9, of just the hands to show exactly what's coming from that enlarger. Put it all together and we get Figure 11, an image I was excited about. From that day's printing I ended up with two versions,

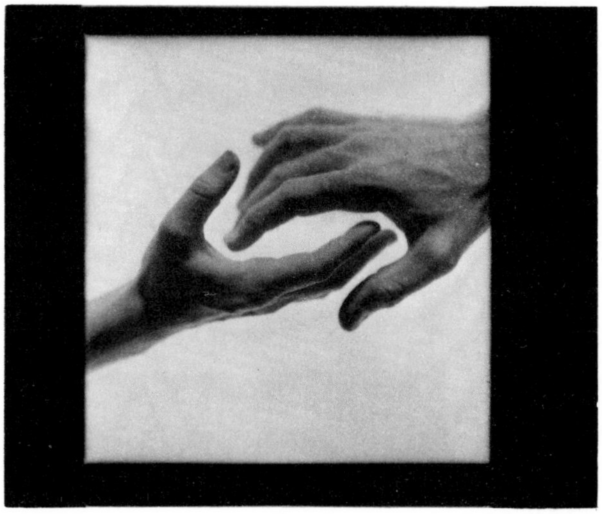

Figure 9.

Figures 10 and 11. They have a similar feel.

Time and again people ask me which image I like best, and I try to avoid this sort of qualitative distinction. Sometimes it's very clear as to which works better, but in this instance, I think that they are equal yet different. I can make a personal case for each of them. I enjoy the tremendous space that exists in the mountain print. You start close and move back into the infinite distance. The anthropomorphic quality of the banyan tree in the other print appeals to me, too. I think of this as my Florida version and the other as my Western version. I don't feel that the content, the particular evocative power of the image, shifts much between the two versions, because the enigma is located in the hands and the rock. The backgrounds are supportive in different ways but I can't make a qualitative distinction there.

A point I want to bring up here is that it's hard to know when you're printing an image what long range value it will have. I've had an image occur in the darkroom and thought, "There's a real winner" and I've printed twenty of them. The next day I wonder why I did it. Then there are times when I've made one print and a week later I had to go back and print more because I liked it so much.

One of the hazards of working this way for a long time is that you begin to pre-visualize your post-visualization. If I start working it out too much, I set up blocks for myself. I go out on a limb to be more casual, because I like the idea of letting the medium have a say in the image as it evolves.

For real growth as an artist, perhaps as a person, you have to move to the fringes of your consciousness, of your understanding. Sometimes these images come with barely intelligible questions. You know that something strange is happening and you want to understand it more clearly, but you're not ready for it. It's asking you to stretch and grow. When I make one print of an image, there's often an element of doubt about where it is leading me. Then I look at the print later and maybe it has sustained, provocative power. This discovery is nurturing, it's where the real growth occurs. When you're more secure about the growth, I suppose you feel more comfortable with the image. It looks like something you've done and something you can be proud of.

There must also be an intuitive trust in yourself, so that you will go with what's coming from inside. And then there's playfulness. I take photography very seriously, but at the same time it's true play. Sometimes when I haven't had much time to print and I get a free day, I think, "Boy, I'd really like to do something fine. I want to produce art today." Well, that's a hell of an attitude to take into the darkroom. Every time that notion enters my head, it takes me quite a while to get rid of, to return to my material, in its purest form.

FILM	ASA RATING	DEVELOPER	SOLUTION & TIME	AGITATION
Plus-X	125	Microdol-X	1:3 / 10½ minutes	Continuous for first 15 seconds / 5 seconds in every minute / Inversion method

ENLARGER	LENS	LIGHT SOURCE	USUAL APERTURE	USUAL EXPOSURE
Omega B8 (3 to 6 enlargers used per print)	Fujinon EP 75mm *f*/5.6	No. 212	*f*/11	10 seconds

PAPER	DEVELOPER	SOLUTION & TIME	STOP BATH	FIXER
Varilour VLTW	LPD	1:2 / 2 minutes	Water	Kodak F-5 / 2 baths / 5 minutes in each

WASH	TONING	DRYING	FLATTENING	PRESENTATION
Tray wash	None	Air dry on fiberglass screen	None	Drymount on 100% rag board / Under plexiglas / Simplest metal strip frame

Figure 10.

Figure 11.